Becoming a Woman of

Simplicity

CYNTHIA HEALD

*I am afraid that, as the serpent deceived Eve by his
craftiness, your minds will be led astray from the
simplicity and purity of devotion to Christ.*
2 Corinthians 11:3, NASB

NAVPRESS

*A NavPress resource published in alliance
with Tyndale House Publishers, Inc.*

NAVPRESS⬤®

NavPress is the publishing ministry of The Navigators, an international Christian organization and leader in personal spiritual development. NavPress is committed to helping people grow spiritually and enjoy lives of meaning and hope through personal and group resources that are biblically rooted, culturally relevant, and highly practical.

For more information, visit www.NavPress.com.

Becoming a Woman of Simplicity

Copyright © 2009 by Cynthia Heald. All rights reserved.

A NavPress resource published in alliance with Tyndale House Publishers, Inc.

Visit the author's website at www.cynthiaheald.com.

NAVPRESS and the NAVPRESS logo are registered trademarks of NavPress, The Navigators, Colorado Springs, CO. *TYNDALE* is a registered trademark of Tyndale House Publishers, Inc. Absence of ® in connection with marks of NavPress or other parties does not indicate an absence of registration of those marks.

The Team:
Don Pape. Publisher
Caitlyn Carlson, Acquisitions Editor
Jennifer Ghionzoli, Designer

Cover vintage border copyright © Vintage Style Designs/Creative Market. All rights reserved.
Cover typeface and floral illustration copyright © Lisa Glanz/Creative Market. All rights reserved.
Cover font by Laura Worthington/Creative Market. All rights reserved.

Author photograph by Shelly Han Photography, copyright © 2016. All rights reserved.

Some of the anecdotal illustrations in this book are true to life and are included with the permission of the persons involved. All other illustrations are composites of real situations, and any resemblance to people living or dead is purely coincidental.

Cataloging-in-Publication Data is available.

ISBN 978-1-60006-663-4

Printed in the United States of America

22   21
15   14   13   12   11

Contents

Preface

SIMPLICITY—A WORD THAT EVOKES wistful sighs and earnest longings for a more ordered and peaceful life—a life where time is considered to be a gift from a benevolent king and not a burden from a harsh taskmaster. Often the demands and challenges of each day spill over into weeks and years lived all too quickly, leaving us spent and sighing for rest, for quiet, for simplicity.

Can life in this multitasking, instantaneous, technologically driven age be tamed? Is it possible to live unpretentiously in a world that clamors for constant communication? Does God's Word address the intricacies of our world? Is it possible to live simply?

Perhaps it is only because I am older that a more tempered pace of life has become appealing, but years spent living on a merry-go-round that tended to never stop has given me a desire to encourage others to live life the way God intended. God invites us to enter into His rest, to receive His peace, and to be still. It doesn't mean that life is not difficult or sometimes overwhelming, but it does mean that we can live with a deep, abiding sense that all is well with our souls.

I believe that simplicity must come from within. When we are inwardly simple—at rest, free, willing to trust—then we can step into a chaotic world and be at peace. A continual growing knowledge and intimacy with God is essential to being able to live a life that can at once be simple but profound enough to confront the recurrent challenges of daily life. Trusting and resting in God grants us inward simplicity that can then lead to an outward simplicity obtained by making wise choices in a complex world.

As you explore this whole idea of simplifying your life, you will discover that God wants you to know His perfect peace, to choose the "best," and to live in the present. You will find biblical principles that will teach you to live simply and purely in devotion to Christ so that you can say with the psalmist, "I have calmed and quieted myself, like a weaned child who no longer cries for its mother's milk. Yes, like a weaned child is my soul within me" (Psalm 131:2).

Blessings as you join me in becoming a woman of simplicity.

Cynthia Heald

Suggestions

–FOR USING THIS STUDY–

THIS STUDY IS DESIGNED FOR both individual as well as small group use, and for women of any age or family status.

Many of the questions will guide you into Scripture passages. Ask God to reveal His truth to you through His Word. Bible study references—such as commentaries and handbooks—can help you understand particular passages by providing historical background, contexts, and common interpretations. (In a few cases you may want to access a standard dictionary for general word definitions.)

Other questions will ask you to reflect on your own life. Approach these questions honestly and thoughtfully; however, if you're doing this study in a group, don't feel that you must reveal private details of your life experiences. Use the reflection questions at the close of each chapter to help you work through significant issues raised by your study. If you keep a personal journal, you might want to write these reflections there rather than in this guide.

Each chapter begins with a foundational Scripture passage for you to memorize. You may memorize the verse before or after doing the chapter study, in any Bible translation you choose. Write the memory verses (from your favorite version) on a card or Post-it, put it in a place where you will see it regularly, and memorize it. Thank God for who He is and for what He is doing in your life.

The quotes from classic thinkers and writers have been carefully selected to enhance your understanding and enjoyment of the content in *Becoming a Woman of Simplicity*. The references for these quotations (see the "Notes" section at the back of the book) will also furnish an excellent reading list for your own devotional reading and study.

There is no leader's guide, but most facilitators stimulate discussion by moving through each chapter section by section and by using the personal application questions placed throughout the study. Providing time for prayer along with a loving and safe environment for women to share their personal insights and challenges will hopefully encourage, unite, and bless each member of the group.

The Child spoke:

Father, I am tired. It seems that I am always tired.

I know, My child. You need rest.

But I don't have time to rest! I can't even get everything
done as it is.

*The rest I speak of is a special rest that only I can give. But you
must come to Me to receive it.*

How long will it take?

It will take a lifetime.

A lifetime? I don't understand.

*My rest is given to those who are willing to give up living life
in their own strength. This means that you allow Me to
be your strength, your Shepherd who will guide you all
the days of your life along the right paths.*

Living in my own strength, is that what I have been doing?

*You have complicated your life by trying to do too much. Your
busyness has kept you from what is essential: your time to
know Me and what I desire for you.*

Is there a simpler way?

*My way is the way of freedom, peace, and rest. My way is the
way of simplicity and purity of devotion to Christ.*

May I have the rest that You give?

Yes. Come, take My yoke.

CHAPTER 1

PROFOUND SIMPLICITY

I am afraid that, as the serpent deceived Eve by his craftiness, your minds will be led astray from the simplicity and purity of devotion to Christ.
2 CORINTHIANS 11:3, NASB

We simplify, not just to be less busy, even though we may be right to pursue that. Rather, we simplify to remove distractions from our pursuit of Christ. We prune activities from our lives, not only to get organized, but also that our devotion to Christ and service for His kingdom will be more fruitful. We simplify, not merely to save time, but to eliminate hindrances to the time we devote to knowing Christ. All the reasons we simplify should eventually lead us to Jesus Christ.
DONALD S. WHITNEY, *Simplify Your Spiritual Life*

I SMILED AS I READ the T-shirt slogan: *I am woman, I am invincible, I am tired.* What an appropriate commentary on our lives as women. We are great multitaskers and have hearts to give and serve, but at the end of the day we are usually weary—weary from the pressures of jobs, family, and commitments. Our schedules dictate our lives, and the demands and needs of everyday life leave us little time for what we truly love and value. We keep thinking that next week, next month it will be better, but often the unexpected barges into our already full lives and our longing for a simpler lifestyle stirs our hearts.

The challenge to live more simply is not new to our generation.

More than fifty years ago, in her book *Gift from the Sea*, Anne Morrow Lindbergh expressed her desire for simplicity:

> There are so few empty pages in my engagement pad, or empty hours in the day, or empty rooms in my life in which to stand alone and find myself. Too many activities, and people, and things. Too many worthy activities, valuable things, and interesting people. For it is not merely the trivial which clutters our lives but the important as well.[1]

We do live in a world of "too many" activities, people, and things. Our years are lived all too quickly and we suddenly realize that our lives lack a quality of significance because there is so little empty space. The challenge of leaving empty pages on our calendars is that so many of the opportunities we encounter are worthy and valuable. But the "too many" has the potential of leading us astray from the most vital aspect of our lives: our devotion to Christ.

As a loving pastor, the apostle Paul wrote to the Corinthian church expressing his concern that false teachers might lure his flock away from the purity and simplicity of their love for Christ. The Greek word for simplicity is *haplotēs*, which means "single-ness, sincerity, without pretense."[2] Paul reminded the Corinthians that just as a betrothed woman should have a singleness of affection for her husband, so should Christians have a single-minded devotion to Christ. The purity he is concerned about is their purity of doctrine. He feared that the church might be led astray from the simple truths that Christ had taught.

This single-minded devotion to Christ is the fundamental principle of this study. My concern is that we live in a world where doing, communicating, and possessing so rule our lives that we have allowed even good things to overtake our time and distract from the best. The purpose of this study is not to show you how to downsize, declutter, or say no to everything. The purpose is to encourage you to live the way God has planned for you. I think His way is one of inner peace and rest in the midst of a complex and busy world. My definition of a woman of simplicity is one who lives a God-paced life. She waits for God's leading, and she has time to be still and know her Lord. She has a deep abiding rest in her spirit. She is a woman of profound simplicity because she has only one focus: being simply and purely devoted to Christ.

GOD'S DESIRE FOR OUR SIMPLICITY

Charles Swindoll has observed, "Noise and words and frenzied, hectic schedules dull our senses, closing our ears to his still, small voice and making us numb to his touch."[3] How can we hear His still, small voice with all that daily life expects of us? Perhaps Psalm 23 is a good beginning to understand God's desire for us. In the first three verses David testifies that the Lord is actively involved in bestowing rest and quiet. *The Message* translates them as,

> GOD, my shepherd!
>   I don't need a thing.
> You have bedded me down in lush meadows,
>   you find me quiet pools to drink from.
> True to your word,
>   you let me catch my breath
>   and send me in the right direction.

What refreshing words for those of us who tend to collapse into bed at the end of each day, who hurriedly buy drinks at drive-through windows, and who rarely have time to catch our breath. This best-known and beloved psalm of David addresses the whole spectrum of our lives: peaceful streams and dark valleys. In our pursuit of simplicity, we hear David succinctly "sing" about God's longing for us to catch our breath.

1. Read Psalm 23 in one or two translations, and as you read write down your answers to these questions:

    a. Jesus proclaimed that He is our Good Shepherd who knows His sheep (see John 10:14). As our Shepherd, what does the Lord desire to provide for you?

    b. Rest and quiet are rare commodities in our world. What, for you, would be lush meadows and quiet pools?

    c. God's provision and personal care are beautifully portrayed in this psalm. What do you sense the Lord is saying to you about what a life lived in single-minded devotion to Him would look like?

"I shall not want. He makes me lie down in green pastures, he leadeth me beside the still waters." His own resources, His own restfulness is shared with His own people. They need have no worries. He undertakes to look after everything. That is something the world cannot give and something it cannot take away.[4]   JOHN PHILLIPS

2. Many of us have walked through dark valleys, but few of us consistently experience the rest the Lord wants to give. It is evident, though, that God wants us to have empty pages, hours, and rooms in our lives.

    a. As you read these Scriptures, record your thoughts about how you may be able to experience spiritual rest.

        PSALM 127:1-2

        ISAIAH 30:15

        MATTHEW 11:28-30

b. Each of these passages gives perspective on living as God intends. Why do you think that we are not willing or able to receive the Lord's quietness and rest?

3. Based on your study so far, how would you evaluate your life in regard to having a restful spirit and a single-minded pursuit of the Lord? Write down what dulls your senses to His still, small voice and what helps you to hear Him as He leads you along the right path.

You have made us for yourself, and our hearts are restless till they find their rest in you.[5]   ST. AUGUSTINE OF HIPPO

GOD'S DESIRE TO LIVE IN US

1. Truly our hearts are restless until we find rest in the Lord. In order to accomplish His desire to give us true rest, God sent His Son to be our Savior and His Spirit to indwell us.

a. What do these verses tell you about Christ living in you?

JOHN 14:23-27 ···

1 CORINTHIANS 1:30 ·····································

1 JOHN 4:13-16 ···

b. Because of Christ's death on the cross, He has made us right with God. All who confess that Jesus is Savior and Lord have God living in them (see Romans 10:9). Take a few minutes to relate how you have experienced Christ living in you.

c. To know of Jesus' great love and sacrifice and His life within us is humbling and amazing. How does this knowledge of His love and presence encourage you to begin to live simply and devotedly for Him?

The theology of the cross simplifies the spiritual life by standing as its primary reference point. Everything in Christian spirituality relates to it. Through the cross we begin our spirituality, and by the power and example of the cross we live it.[6]
                         DONALD S. WHITNEY

2. As you seek to receive God's rest and to live sincerely in devotion to Christ, what do you learn from these key verses about ways that you can experience rest and simplify your life?

PSALM 37:7

PSALM 46:10

MATTHEW 6:33

The Message translation of Psalm 46:10 says, "Step out of the traffic! Take a long, loving look at me, your High God." Consider what this means to you. What is one practical way that you can begin to step out of the traffic?

THOUGHTS AND REFLECTIONS FROM AN OLDER WOMAN

When I am asked to describe my ministry, I answer by saying that I believe God wants me to be an older woman (I certainly qualify!) who teaches younger women. In this study I want to be your older woman to hopefully teach you good things (see Titus 2:3-5).

In 1964 a dear older woman encouraged me to live wholly devoted to Christ. This became my heart's desire, but I didn't realize that my life would revolve around a husband (who was a busy veterinarian), four children, and a myriad of opportunities to serve. I was involved in worthy things: helping in my children's schools and activities, being in a garden club, serving in Sunday school, teaching a Bible study, inviting friends over for a meal. All of these activities were good, but my problem was that I was committed to doing them all at the same time.

As a result I felt pulled in many directions and eventually realized that I was missing out on what was most important. My busy life was robbing me of my most precious relationships—my time with the Lord and my family. When it dawned on me that the highlight of my day was falling into bed at night, I knew I needed to change the way I was living.

A verse in John 15 penetrated my heart and made all the difference in my learning to live as God desires. John 15:5 says, "Yes, I am the vine; you are the branches. Those who remain in me, and I in them, will produce much fruit. For apart from me you can do nothing." The last few words really challenged me: apart from Christ, I essentially could do nothing. I was doing a lot of good things, but they were taking the place of the most important. I needed to abide—to stay connected to the Lord by taking His yoke and walking with Him throughout each day.

Abiding is not an activity; it is a lifestyle. It is reordering my whole perspective on life so that my sole purpose is to live simply and purely in devotion to the Lord. It is letting the Lord be my Shepherd who leads me along right paths. It is seeking first His Kingdom and His righteousness. It is being still and waiting patiently for the Lord by spending special time with Him, sitting at His feet, and reading His Word. Abiding allows the Lord to bring interesting people, worthy activities, and valuable things into my life in the right way, at the right time, and for His purpose. Because the Lord is my Shepherd I am prompted to prune activities and eliminate hindrances that would draw me away from Christ. My abiding, taking His yoke and walking at His pace on His path for me, has profoundly shaped my life, and as an older woman I want to encourage you to seek this same intimacy with the Lord.

As you begin your journey of becoming a woman of simplicity, you can start by trusting God to lead you and to provide for all your needs. You can take His yoke in order to maintain a consistent and ever-deepening walk with God. You can set your heart to let the Lord be your Shepherd so that you can experience the joy of living simply and purely in devotion to Christ.

PERSONAL THOUGHTS AND REFLECTIONS

Meister Eckhart observed, "The very best and utmost of attainment in this life is to remain still and let God act and speak in thee."[7] It is essential as you begin this study that you plan for a quiet time to be still before the Lord. He wants to lead you by peaceful streams. The time does not need to be long, but it does need to be in a place where you can sit quietly, read His Word, and listen for God's thoughts in your heart. Write down not only what insights or thoughts God might give to you but also your desire to become a woman of simplicity who rests and abides in Christ.

He now not only says, "Come unto me," but "Take my yoke upon you and learn of me"; become my scholars, yield yourselves to my training, submit in all things to my will, let your whole life be one with mine—in other words, Abide in me. And then He adds, not only, "I will give," but "ye shall find rest to your souls."[8] ANDREW MURRAY

SCRIPTURE MEMORY

2 CORINTHIANS 11:3—*I am afraid that, as the serpent deceived Eve by his craftiness, your minds will be led astray from the simplicity and purity of devotion to Christ. (NASB)*

CHAPTER 2

GRACIOUS ACCEPTANCE

God saved you by his grace when you believed. And you can't take credit for this; it is a gift from God. Salvation is not a reward for the good things we have done, so none of us can boast about it. For we are God's masterpiece. He has created us anew in Christ Jesus, so we can do the good things he planned for us long ago.
EPHESIANS 2:8-10

It requires the greatest effort and produces the greatest humility to receive anything from God; we would much sooner earn it.
OSWALD CHAMBERS, *Conformed to His Image*

WITH A SMILE ON HER face, Claire proclaimed, "I have finally realized that I don't *have* to do anything to be valuable to God. He loves me for just who I am." I gave her a hug and thought of how it is indeed a wonderful, freeing revelation to grasp God's grace and acceptance of us so that we are not continually burdened with trying to earn our salvation.

Like many of us, Claire had struggled for years with the concept of God's acceptance of her. She persevered in her serving, working to be sure that she had God's approval. She felt unworthy of His love and so she was willing to do anything she thought might please Him. But she could never be sure that she did enough. As a result, she was tired, not only physically, but spiritually. Her identity was based on her performance—what she *did* defined who she was. She wasn't free to let the Lord lead her by peaceful streams; she wasn't free to enjoy the Shepherd of her soul—she had to work. She could not recognize the gracious acceptance bestowed upon her by her heavenly Father. "Doing" to earn acceptance robbed her of a life of rest and simplicity.

In order to become women of simplicity we must believe that we are saved by God's grace and that we can do nothing to obtain this gracious gift. If our service for the Lord does not spring from grace, then we become overly busy and stressed. On the other hand, grace greatly simplifies our lives. In accepting His grace and the realization that we have become a new creation in Christ, then and only then can we begin to do the good things He planned for us long ago. When we abide and concentrate on the Lord, He renews our strength, and we are led and equipped to do what He desires for us. He is our Shepherd who guides us along the right paths. All we need to do is learn to follow His lead.

❧ GOD'S GRACIOUS ACCEPTANCE

Max Lucado wrote, "You are saved, not because of what you do, but because of what Christ did. And you are special, not because of what you do, but because of whose you are. And you are his."[1] God's grace is His unmerited favor toward us.

1. What insights do you gain from these verses about the basis of God's acceptance of you?

    JOHN 1:12-13

EPHESIANS 1:3-8 ···

EPHESIANS 2:8-9 ···

TITUS 3:4-7 ···

Thomas à Kempis wrote, "They travel lightly whom God's grace carries."[2] As you consider what God's gracious acceptance and Christ's love and sacrifice mean to you, how can His grace help you to travel lightly?

GOD'S GRACIOUS PARTNERSHIP

It is by grace that we are saved and we are created to join Him in the good things He has planned for us. *The Message* states Ephesians 2:8-10 in this way:

Saving is all his idea, and all his work. All we do is trust him enough to let him do it. It's God's gift from start to finish! We don't play the major role. If we did, we'd probably go around bragging that we'd done the whole thing! No, we neither make nor save ourselves. God does both the making and saving. He creates each of us by Christ Jesus to join him in the work he does, the good work he has gotten ready for us to do, work we had better be doing.

Once we accept that salvation is free and cannot be earned, we are then free to do what truly pleases the Lord. It is not that we don't do anything; it's that what we do is the good work of God.

2. What do these Scriptures say to you about working for God's good pleasure?

EPHESIANS 2:10

PHILIPPIANS 2:12-13

TITUS 3:8

Good works are part of God's plan. They are not the price *of salvation, but the* proof. *The believer is not saved as a result of good works; good works are the result of salvation. They are the result of God's working in the believer's heart. They are the evidence that he is alive from the dead. They are the proof of the glorious togetherness that exists between the believer and the Savior.*[3]   JOHN PHILLIPS

TAKING CHRIST'S YOKE

3. If we want to be sure that we are concentrating on God, then we need to be certain that we are connected to Christ. Read Matthew 11:28-30 again. As you study this passage, write down how taking Christ's yoke can enable you to do the good things God has planned for you.

Consider *The Message* translation of this verse (Matthew 11:29): "Walk with me and work with me—watch how I do it. Learn the unforced rhythms of grace." I really like the phrase *unforced rhythms of grace.* This is what God is after—our acceptance of His grace so that we live as He intends. If you truly respond to Christ's call and take His yoke, how will your life and service be different?

❧ ACCEPTING THAT WE ARE GOD'S MASTERPIECE

Some Bible translations phrase Ephesians 2:10 as, "We are His workmanship, created in Christ Jesus for good works." John Phillips observes, "The word translated 'workmanship,' *poiēma*, indicates that we are His poem, His masterpiece. Each of our lives is the canvas on which the Master is producing a work of art that will fill the everlasting ages with His praise."[4] It is God who created us and takes responsibility for our lives; therefore as His child, we can trust Him to lead us.

4. David understood this concept and wrote an extraordinary psalm depicting a child at rest. Psalm 131 is one of my favorites. Read it several times and record your observations concerning the issues David confronted in order to calm and quiet his soul.

It is David's choice to compose his soul—to rest in the Lord. How does his description of the weaned child help you to understand what it is to be at rest?

His heart is not lifted up; his eyes do not look enviously and hungrily to the heights beyond him; he does not dwell in anxious, wearisome thought on matters which are best left alone; he concentrates his sympathies and his energies on that which demands his attention, and which is productive of good to himself and those around him; he is perfectly contented to be just what God has made him, to go where his Master sends him, to do what is placed in his hands to do. He is so far from thinking himself essential to the prosperity of the Church and the redemption of the world, that he hopefully, and even confidently, leaves that in the care of the Supreme.[5] E. R. CONDER AND W. CLARKSON

5. In God's great love and kindness He calls us to be His children. How does the knowledge of God's gracious acceptance affect your perception of how you are to serve Him?

Beware of any work for God that causes or allows you to avoid concentrating on Him. A great number of Christian workers worship their work. The only concern of Christian workers should be their concentration on God.[6]

OSWALD CHAMBERS

THOUGHTS AND REFLECTIONS
FROM AN OLDER WOMAN

I love God because He has graciously purchased our salvation and then works within us to accomplish His good pleasure. God's love is unconditional, and He wants us to be free from the burden of feeling that we must work for His acceptance and instead be free to do the good things He has planned for us. Otherwise we will either begin to worship our work or allow our work to become burdensome.

I smiled when I read Conder and Clarkson's statement about David being so at rest that he realized he was not essential to the prosperity of the church and the redemption of the world. So many times I've wrestled with responding to many of the needs of the church: teaching Sunday school, helping in the nursery, serving in women's ministry, volunteering as church treasurer. Whenever I heard of a need at the Gospel Rescue Mission, I struggled with juggling my commitments so I could serve the homeless. I wanted to take on all of these good things, but in reality I think I was seeking to prove my acceptability to God by what I could *do* for Him. Yet because of the season of life I was in, my family and other responsibilities required the majority of my time.

I remember the time when I left my very young children with a babysitter in order to go read to children in a Head Start program. God patiently but firmly spoke to my heart, *Cynthia, there will be time someday for you to serve in this way, but for now I would rather you stay home and read to your own children.*

This was a turning point for me. I came to realize that ministry from God's perspective could be to my family or wherever

He happened to place me at the time. Because He knows that my heart is to serve Him—to work *out* the results of my salvation— He continues to confirm in my heart that I am valuable to Him and that He is capable of guiding me and placing me where He wants me to serve. Philippians 2:13 is true: "God is working in you, giving you the desire and the power to do what pleases him."

The key to knowing what I should be doing is my being yoked to Christ. It is in walking daily with Him that I can hear His voice. The question is whether I will listen to what He is asking me to do or not to do. Early in my Christian life, I read the booklet *Tyranny of the Urgent*. Charles Hummel's premise is that often we allow an urgent need to take us away from what is important. He writes,

> Prayerful waiting on God is indispensable to effective service. . . . The need itself is not the call; the call must come from the God who knows our limitations. . . .
> It is not God who loads us until we bend or crack with an ulcer, nervous breakdown, heart attack, or stroke. These come from our inner compulsions coupled with the pressure of circumstances.[7]

Prayerful waiting on God can only occur when I am abiding and concentrating on Him. Knowing that I am not required to meet all the needs that I hear about has been a blessed and guiding truth. It is only when I pray and wait for God to lead me that I can discern His way. I either hear His voice in my heart saying, *"This is the way, walk in it"* (Isaiah 30:21, NASB), or I have a sense of peace about what I should do. If God does call me to minister in a certain area, then His grace will be sufficient and my strength will be renewed. I must always be alert, though, for I can easily fall back into choosing to serve in order to meet a need in my own life or because I want to please people. If any service begins to replace my spending time with God or if I become overly burdened and burned out, then I need to reevaluate my ministry.

Oswald Chambers, my favorite author, says it simply: "This is your line of service—to see that there is nothing between Jesus and yourself."[8] Until I am wholeheartedly walking with God, He is not able to accomplish the special work He has for me. When I am abiding, then I no longer have to wonder if I am doing enough. God's plan is simple: He takes responsibility for my life and service; I take responsibility to maintain my concentration on God. And when there is nothing between Jesus and me, I can calm and quiet my soul and serve simply and purely in devotion to Christ.

❦ PERSONAL THOUGHTS AND REFLECTIONS

God's gracious acceptance frees us to live profoundly and simply because we can rest in Him and know that He is at work in us to give us the desire and power to do what pleases Him. Take time away to be still and let the Lord "speak to thee" about why and how you serve Him and how you have accepted His acceptance. Write down not only what insights and thoughts He gives you, but also your desire to learn the "unforced rhythms of grace" as you serve Him. The Christian is

> not like an infant crying loudly for his mother's breast, but like a weaned child that quietly rests by his mother's side, happy in being with her. . . . No desire now comes between

him and his God; for he is sure that God knows what he needs before he asks him. And just as the child gradually breaks off the habit of regarding his mother only as a means of satisfying his own desires and learns to love her for her own sake, so the worshipper after a struggle has reached an attitude of mind in which he desires God for himself and not as a means of fulfillment of his own wishes. His life's centre of gravity has shifted. He now rests no longer in himself but in God.[9]

ARTUR WEISER

SCRIPTURE MEMORY

EPHESIANS 2:8-10—*God saved you by his grace when you believed. And you can't take credit for this; it is a gift from God. Salvation is not a reward for the good things we have done, so none of us can boast about it. For we are God's masterpiece. He has created us anew in Christ Jesus, so we can do the good things he planned for us long ago.*

CHAPTER 3

"THE WORLD IS TOO MUCH WITH US"

Do not love this world nor the things it offers you, for when you love the world, you do not have the love of the Father in you.

1 JOHN 2:15

We Christians must simplify our lives or lose untold treasures on earth and in eternity. Modern civilization is so complex as to make the devotional life all but impossible. It wears us out by multiplying distractions and beats us down by destroying our solitude, where otherwise we might drink and renew our strength before going out to face the world again.

A. W. TOZER, *The Best of A. W. Tozer*

ALTHOUGH THIS POEM BY WILLIAM Wordsworth was written in the early 1800s, it is still relevant to our lives today—

The world is too much with us; late and soon,
Getting and spending, we lay waste our powers:
Little we see in Nature that is ours;
We have given our hearts away, a sordid boon![1]

Wordsworth laments our plight by saying that with all our getting and spending, we have given our hearts away. Because this is our tendency, God's Word clearly addresses our dilemma by reminding us not to love the world's ways or the world's goods, for when we do, we sacrifice our love for our Father. John cautions us because "the world around us is under the control of the evil one" (1 John 5:19). The evil one delights in distracting us—whether it is preoccupation with an abundance of possessions or filling the world with technology that leaves little time to rest quietly in green meadows. How much we need to remember that this world is not our permanent home; we are only passing through (see Hebrews 13:14).

I often think of my grandmother who was born in 1892. She never had to stand in front of her closet and decide what to wear, for she had only two or three dresses and a couple pairs of shoes. She was not stressed about her appearance or her possessions. Her world was small, ours is large. Her world was slow, ours is fast. Her world was essentially peaceful, ours is chaotic. Her world was basic, ours is complex. Her world was not perfect, but at least it did not constantly intrude into her life and continually challenge her to find peace and rest.

Wordsworth is right—getting and spending do lay waste to our powers and we see little in nature that is ours because we have so little time to stop. Because the world is too much with us, we need "to simplify our lives or lose untold treasures on earth and in eternity."

IN, BUT NOT OF, THE WORLD

1. Before Jesus was arrested He prayed for His disciples and for us. One of His requests addressed our connection to the world. As you read the Scriptures below, consider how you should relate to the world. Record your observations.

JOHN 17:13-19

JAMES 4:4-8

Our Lord did not teach detachment from other things: He taught attachment to Himself. Jesus Christ was not a recluse. He did not cut Himself off from society; He was amazingly in and out among the ordinary things of life; but He was disconnected fundamentally from it all. He was not aloof, but He lived in another world.[2]

OSWALD CHAMBERS

LIVING IN THE WORLD GOD'S WAY

2. In His Sermon on the Mount, Jesus taught specifically about how much thought we should give to providing for our physical needs. Carefully read Matthew 6:19-34 and in your own words summarize Jesus' teaching about what your perspective should be concerning your necessities and possessions.

Jesus encourages you to have faith in God's daily provision. Why do you think that He emphasizes not being worried or anxious about your everyday life? (Note particularly verse 33.)

Matthew Henry makes this observation based on the King James Version of Matthew 6:25: "Take no thought for your life."

But the *thought* here forbidden is . . . a disquieting, tormenting *thought*, which hurries the mind hither and thither, and hangs it in suspense; which disturbs our joy in God, and is a damp upon our hope in him; which breaks the sleep, and hinders our enjoyment of ourselves, of our friends, and of what God has given us. . . . A distrustful, unbelieving *thought*. God has promised to provide for those that are his all things needful for life and

godliness, *the life that now is*, food and a covering; not
dainties, but necessaries.[3]   MATTHEW HENRY

3. Four times in one sermon Jesus said not to be anxious. Paul
    also reminded us not to worry. Read Philippians 4:6-7 and
    write down the blessing you can receive when you have this
    response to anxiety.

4. In Jesus' parable of the farmer sowing the seed of God's Word,
    He mentions the seed that fell among thorns. As you read Mark
    4:18-19, note the reason that this seed did not bear fruit.

Our fruitfulness depends on how we receive His message (see
verse 20) and our awareness that the world can easily crowd out
His Word. Take a moment to evaluate your life to determine
what tends to make you unfruitful. Prayerfully consider either
how you can begin to confront these *hindrances* or your resolve
to continue to resist the world and become more fruitful. Record
your conclusion.

5. The apostle Paul succinctly stated his relationship with the world. Listen to his words in Galatians: "Because of that cross, my interest in this world has been crucified, and the world's interest in me has also died. . . . What counts is whether we have been transformed into a new creation" (Galatians 6:14-15). Paul instantly dealt a deathblow to his interest in the world and firmly placed his focus on what is important: the transforming work of the Holy Spirit.

    The Message translates verse 14 as, "For my part, I am going to boast about nothing but the Cross of our Master, Jesus Christ. Because of that Cross, I have been crucified in relation to the world, set free from the stifling atmosphere of pleasing others and fitting into the little patterns that they dictate."

    a. Paul stated that he no longer was interested in the world and its values, but in being transformed. As you read Romans 12:1-2 and Ephesians 4:17-24 write down your insights on the best way to relate to the world as a new creation in Christ.

    b. Spiritual transformation begins in the mind and the heart. When our hearts are set on walking in devotion to Christ, we will be transformed as we abide. In what ways is God's Word encouraging you to be transformed?

c. Not only must we be aware of the material world surrounding us, but we must also be alert to the people in the world. How do you respond to people who, knowingly or unknowingly, tend to pressure you to live according to the world's values?

The world had never known a man like Jesus—absolutely good, unfailingly gracious, the visible expression of the invisible God. And what was the world's answer? A cross.

As the cross was the world's answer to Christ, so the cross is the believer's answer to the world. The world will sometimes mask its face and pretend friendship for the Christian. It will offer us its pleasures, money, methods, and applause—but always at the price of compromise. The Christian's answer is the cross.[4]

JOHN PHILLIPS

THOUGHTS AND REFLECTIONS FROM AN OLDER WOMAN

Daily we encounter a potent enemy. The world brazenly imposes its values on its citizens—wealth, success, productivity, ambition, pride, and busyness. Calendars and clocks rule while possessions, phones, and computers clamor for attention. Maggie Jackson, author of *Distracted*, tells of a father who describes his daughter as being "surgically connected" to her cell phone.[5] My concern is that because the world is too much with us, we easily forfeit the blessing of living a God-paced life that has time for solitude and respite from our noisy world. It is our time spent quietly in His presence that transforms our minds and renews our strength to go back into the world to be the women He wants us to be.

One way to have more discretionary time is to make hard choices concerning our possessions. Jesus taught, "Beware! Guard against every kind of greed. Life is not measured by how much you own" (Luke 12:15). I'm reminded of my friend Marcia, who, because of her husband's work, had to temporarily leave her home of many years and live for an extended time in a small, furnished apartment. They took only a few necessities. After a couple of weeks, I called her to find out how she was coping with her new "smaller" life. Enthusiastically she replied, "Cynthia, I can't believe it. It takes me only thirty minutes to clean the apartment and I'm amazed that I don't miss all the 'things' I thought I needed before the move. I have so much more time now."

It's true, less stuff means more time. Even prominent home decorators tell us that less is more. I like this quotation from a lecture given in 1877 by William Morris, "Have nothing in your houses that you do not know to be useful, or believe to be beautiful."[6]

I like Psalm 4:6-8 from *The Message*:

Why is everyone hungry for more? "More, more," they say.
"More, more."
I have God's more-than-enough,
More joy in one ordinary day

Than they get in all their shopping sprees.
At day's end I'm ready for sound sleep,
For you, GOD, have put my life back together.

Scripture teaches us that love for the world can easily replace our love for the Father. This is why Jesus taught us to seek first His kingdom. Only when our hearts are set on the things of God are we able to respond in the right way to the lure of the world. Only when we trust God to provide for us can we be free from worry. Only when we allow the Spirit to renew our thoughts and attitudes can we be in the world but not of it. It is so tempting to love what the world loves, but when we do yield, we miss out on sound sleep and having God put our lives back together on a daily basis—we miss out on living a life of pure and simple devotion to Christ.

PERSONAL THOUGHTS AND REFLECTIONS

A true understanding of how we are to live in the world is crucial to living profoundly and simply. We become aware of how the world can squeeze us into its mold and keep us busy and occupied so that we have no time to receive God's rest or peace. Take time and let the Lord speak to you about how you relate to the world or allow the world to conform you to its way of doing things. Write down your insights and also your desire to live simply and purely rather than merely copying the world's behavior.

We are not here to possess the world. We are here to show, by how we use the world, that Christ is more precious than the world.[7]

JOHN PIPER

❦ SCRIPTURE MEMORY

1 JOHN 2:15—*Do not love this world nor the things it offers you, for when you love the world, you do not have the love of the Father in you.*

CHAPTER 4

❧ UNSHAKABLE SIMPLICITY ❧

I've told you all this so that trusting me, you will be unshakable and assured, deeply at peace. In this godless world you will continue to experience difficulties. But take heart! I've conquered the world.

JOHN 16:33, MSG

Nothing influences the quality of our life more than how we respond to trouble.

ERWIN G. TIEMAN, *The Westminster Collection of Christian Quotations*

JEANIE, A LONGTIME FRIEND, WAS married later in life. It was an extra-special day for everyone. Shortly after the honeymoon, her husband was in the hospital for routine surgery, but while there he suffered a massive hemorrhage. The doctors gave little hope, and for twelve days his life hung in the balance. How quickly Jeanie's world changed! One moment she was a new bride, and the next she faced the prospect of becoming a widow.

Not only is the world too much with us in terms of enticing us to acquire more and to adopt its values, our world abounds with tribulation and difficulties—over which we have no control. Trials invade our lives unexpectedly and rip the empty pages from our calendars. Some of the crises are minor, some much more catastrophic, but all are stressful. At these times we need an unshakable simplicity in our response to the disruptions, the heartaches, and the pain. Concerning this, Oswald Chambers wrote, "The test of the life of a saint is not success, but faithfulness in human life as it actually is."[1]

And life as it actually is can be hard. Over the years I have been asked my opinion on naming the most pressing problem women face. Initially I answered by enumerating challenges that deeply affect women, such as abuse, divorce, single parenting, pressing finances, sickness, or other overwhelming responsibilities. It was difficult to single out just one area. Recently I was asked again, and as I thought about my answer, I finally said, "The greatest challenge women face is life—life that not only brings joy, but also pain and uncertainty."

Jesus told us that in this godless world we will continue to experience difficulties. Because life is not trouble-free or predictable, I feel that we must study how a woman of simplicity responds to adversity. It would be easy to think that a simple life should not include a lot of problems, but as we know, that is not true. That would not be life as it actually is. The original title for this chapter was "Stress Is a Given." I think it is important to understand that choosing to live simply devoted to the Lord does equip and enable us to remain unshakable in the midst of stressful and trying circumstances.

TAKING HEART

1. Since we will encounter trials and sorrows, it is comforting to know that Jesus has overcome the world. What can you learn from the following verses about why you can take heart in the midst of hard times?

MATTHEW 7:24-27 ....

JOHN 10:27-30 ....

JOHN 16:33 ....

ROMANS 8:35-39 ....

———————————— ⌀ ————————————

Once you are rooted in reality, nothing can shake you. If your faith is in experiences, anything that happens is likely to upset that faith. But nothing can ever change God or the reality of redemption. Base your faith on that, and you are as eternally secure as God Himself. Once you have a personal relationship with Jesus Christ, you will never be moved again.[2]   OSWALD CHAMBERS

2. Oswald Chambers reminds us that we can have an unshakable faith rooted in the redemption given to us by Jesus. Because of our faith and relationship with Christ, we have the ability to respond to adversity God's way. How can the message of these verses help you respond to trials?

ROMANS 5:1-5 ....

JAMES 1:2-8 ....

1 PETER 1:3-9 ....

Rejoicing in trials is contrary to our way of thinking. Write down your understanding of why you are to rejoice when you encounter problems and trials.

All people—believers as well as unbelievers—experience
anxiety, frustration, heartache and disappointment. Some
suffer intense physical pain and catastrophic tragedies. But
that which should distinguish the suffering of believers from
unbelievers is the confidence that our suffering is under the
control of an all-powerful and all-loving God; our suffering
has meaning and purpose in God's eternal plan, and He
brings or allows to come into our lives only that which is for
His glory and our good.[3]   JERRY BRIDGES

KEEPING AN ETERNAL PERSPECTIVE

3. The apostle Paul endured extraordinary trials, but he never
    lost heart. He wrote, "We are pressed on every side by troubles,
    but we are not crushed" (2 Corinthians 4:8). Because he had
    a pure and simple devotion to Christ, he endured. Read
    2 Corinthians 4:13-18 to determine why Paul never gave up
    hope. Record your insights.

4. Psalm 73 is one of my favorites. The psalmist Asaph wrote
    of his struggle in seeing the wicked prosper while he had
    "nothing but trouble all day long; every morning brings [him]
    pain" (verse 14). Asaph then went into the sanctuary of God to

understand the destiny of the wicked. Read verses 21-26 and record his conclusions.

Knowing that God is the strength of your heart and keeping an eternal perspective are essential aspects of enduring trials. How do verses 21-26 encourage you to persevere?

—— ⌇ ——

Life can be horrible, horrible beyond enduring, the pits. But the secret of grace is that it can be all right at the center even when it's all wrong on the edges. For at the center where life is open to the Creator and Savior God, we are held, led, loved, cared for and inseparably bound into the future that he has for every child that he claims as his.[4]

LEWIS SMEDES

GOD'S FAITHFULNESS

5. As we abide in Christ, we are able to maintain a strong "center" in order to receive His daily care and comfort. What

do you learn about how to cope with trials from the following Scriptures?

PSALM 55:22 ....

LAMENTATIONS 3:22-24 ....

MATTHEW 6:34...

———————————— ⌒⌒ ————————————

It has been well said that no man ever sank under the burden of the day. It is when tomorrow's burden is added to the burden of today that the weight is more than a man can bear. Never load yourselves so. . . . If you find yourselves so loaded, at least remember this: it is your own doing, not God's. He begs you to leave the future to him, and mind the present.[5]   GEORGE MACDONALD

6. Psalm 23 emphasizes that when we walk through dark valleys, God is with us. As you review the passages in this chapter, summarize how these truths can help you to be unshakable.

THOUGHTS AND REFLECTIONS FROM AN OLDER WOMAN

Often I have had the privilege of observing how the people around me respond to trials. When the storm of her husband's brush with death came, Jeanie was certainly concerned and apprehensive, but she did not collapse, because Jesus is the center of her life. Over the years she has built her house on solid rock. Her spirit was sustained and strengthened, and she was able to remain unshakable throughout the slow recovery of her husband.

My friend Danna had her patience and faith tested when her bank misplaced her deposit. This oversight precipitated countless phone calls and hours of work to clear charges for the supposed insufficient funds. To be sure, this was a minor crisis, but it added stress and robbed her of time. She told me that she struggled with her responses to the various people she had to deal with, but she knew in her heart that being gracious was more important than venting her frustrations. It was important for her testimony with others, and it was best for her own soul. She knew Proverbs 11:17, "Your own soul is nourished when you are kind" (TLB). Certainly the quality of our lives is greatly influenced by how we respond to trouble.

Jesus teaches that each day's trouble is enough for that day. *The Message* translates Matthew 6:34 by saying,

Give your entire attention to what God is doing right now, and don't get worked up about what may or may not happen tomorrow. God will help you deal with whatever hard things come up when the time comes.

My dear, older friend Mary wrote a sweet letter to me relating how she had learned this truth. Here is part of her note: "At that time I had a daughter dying of cancer, a son in prison, a husband with Parkinson's, and a precious older single sister in an adult care home. I was the one responsible for all the decisions regarding her situation. We were always close and I was happy to do that for her, but sometimes the weight of it all combined seemed more than I could bear. And in fact, it was more than *I* could bear, until one night in the middle of the night when I couldn't sleep; I went out to the living room to cry out to God. And in His great faithfulness, He reminded me of Matthew 6:34 and the Spirit seemed to say to me, *Your problem is that you are on overload because of the future—God's command is to take one day at a time.* I turned a corner that night, and I've made a constant effort to stay on that path. I truly cannot fathom any other way to survive all of life's uncertainties."[6]

I can abide in Christ, I can follow the Shepherd of my soul, I can live devoted to Christ, but it will not keep me, my family, or my friends from experiencing heartache. Tribulation and stress are a given while we are here on earth. My desire is to be faithful in life as it actually is, to rejoice not in the trials, but in the good that God can bring from my patient endurance. I have found that the only way I can remain unshakable, assured, and deeply at peace is when I take heart from being in the presence of Christ. The only way I can experience His mercies to live just for today is to sit at

His feet and listen to His Word. While abiding in Him I receive the strength, the wisdom, and the eternal perspective I need to respond to adversity in order not to be led astray from the simplicity and purity of devotion to Christ.

PERSONAL THOUGHTS AND REFLECTIONS

How you respond to trials does affect the quality of your life. Difficulties in themselves are hard enough to endure, but the wrong reaction tends to compound your distress. Take time and let the Lord speak to you about how you handle hardship and what you might need to do for your endurance to grow. Write down the insights He gives you and also your desire for God's wisdom and strength to live in single-hearted devotion to Christ in the midst of affliction.

We can be sure that the development of a beautiful Christlike character will not occur in our lives without adversity. . . . We may think we have true Christian love until someone offends us or treats us unjustly. Then we begin to see anger and resentment well up within us. We may conclude we have learned about genuine Christian joy until our lives are shattered by an unexpected calamity or grievous disappointment. Adversities spoil our peace and sorely try our patience. God uses those difficulties to reveal to us our need to grow, so that we will reach out to Him to change us more and more into the likeness of His Son.[7]   JERRY BRIDGES

SCRIPTURE MEMORY

JOHN 16:33—*I've told you all this so that trusting me, you will be unshakable and assured, deeply at peace. In this godless world you will continue to experience difficulties. But take heart! I've conquered the world.* (MSG)

CHAPTER 5

⟨ THIS ONE THING I DO ⟩

I do not regard myself as having laid hold of it yet; but one thing I do:
forgetting what lies behind and reaching forward to what lies ahead,
I press on toward the goal for the prize of the upward call of God in
Christ Jesus.
PHILIPPIANS 3:13-14, NASB (emphasis added)

There is only one relationship that matters, and that is your personal
relationship to a personal Redeemer and Lord. Let everything else go,
but maintain that at all costs, and God will fulfil His purpose through
your life.
OSWALD CHAMBERS, *My Utmost for His Highest*

I LIKE "ONE" THINGS. WHEN someone says, "Here is the one thing you need to do," I listen because I think, *Okay, I can probably handle one thing.* So when Paul said, "But one thing I do," I quickly looked to find out what this godly man was exerting all his efforts in doing. In recounting his past as a Pharisee, he told how he had kept the law without fault and had even harshly persecuted the church. Then he met Christ on the Damascus Road and everything changed. He wrote, "But whatever things were gain to me, those things I have counted as loss for the sake of Christ. More than that, I count all things to be loss in view of the surpassing value of knowing Christ Jesus my Lord" (Philippians 3:7-8, NASB).

Paul wrote this letter to the Philippians probably thirty years after his first encounter with Christ. Even though Paul had known the Lord for many years, he wanted to continue to grow deeper in his knowledge of Jesus. Robert Lightner tells us, "Paul already knew Christ as his Savior. But he wanted to know Him more intimately as his Lord. *To know* (verse 10) means 'to know by experience' (*gnōnai*)."[1] Paul's goal and passion were to know Jesus, not by gaining more information, but by personally experiencing His presence. Paul was willing to give up everything in order to become one with Christ. Paul had a single-minded devotion to his Lord. This was his one thing.

D. L. Moody, a man busy in the work of Christ, was quoted as saying, "It is better to say, 'This one thing I do,' than to say, 'These forty things I dabble with.'"[2]

❦ GOD IS SEEKING US

1. As our Father, God wants us to know Him. Andrew Murray stated, "The relationship He seeks to establish is an intensely personal one: it hinges on the two little words *I* and *You*."[3] What do these verses tell you about knowing God?

PSALM 46:10-11 .... ꕥ

ISAIAH 43:10-13 .... ꙩ

COLOSSIANS 1:9-10 .... ꙩ

——————————— ꙩ ———————————

But God wills our good, and our good is to love Him . . .
and to love Him we must know Him: and if we know Him,
we shall in fact fall on our faces. . . . Yet the call is not only
to prostration and awe; it is to a reflection of the Divine life,
a creaturely participation in the Divine attributes which
is far beyond our present desires. We are bidden to "put on
Christ," to become like God. That is, whether we like it
or not, God intends to give us what we need, not what we
now think we want. Once more, we are embarrassed by the
intolerable compliment, by too much love, not too little.[4]

C. S. LEWIS

OUR SEEKING GOD

2. An essential aspect in knowing God is being still before Him.
    John Phillips reminds us, "We cannot know God if we are

rushing here and there, with countless calls pulling us in various directions. . . . We must 'take time to be holy,' to get to know our Lord as a person with whom we delight to spend time."⁵ A biblical example of one who needed to be still was Martha.

a. Read Luke 10:38-42 and write down your observations about how differently Mary and Martha related to Jesus.

b. Here Jesus said there is only one thing to be concerned about. Perhaps we should listen! How would you describe the one thing Mary had chosen?

c. Martha's heart was to serve the Lord; she loved Him, yet Scripture tells us that Martha was distracted by all her preparations. Where would you be if you had been in Martha and Mary's home? Explain.

Jesus says something extraordinary about what Mary did: it would become a permanent part of her life; it would count for eternity. Quite a promise.

And what did Mary do? All she did was sit. It was where she sat that made the difference.[6]　　KEN GIRE

3. Seeking and knowing the Lord should be our focus and goal. How do these verses encourage you to wholehearted devotion?

PSALM 27:1-6 ....

PSALM 84:10 ....

PHILIPPIANS 3:7-11 ....

In David's case, his battles were won in his private times of worship with the Lord. David had many responsibilities, and there were many demands upon his time; but his number one priority was seeking God's face. He said, like Paul, "This one thing I do" (Phil. 3:13). Without satisfying worship, there can be no successful warfare. How did David know that God was a light, a deliverer, and a fortress? He learned it while gazing on God's glory in his time of worship and meditation. . . . How he longed to leave the battlefield and dwell in God's house! But, wherever he was, he took time to come into God's presence, meditate on God's gracious kindness and contemplate the person of God.[7]

WARREN WIERSBE

4. A warrior king and a persevering apostle had the same goal: to know God. David and Paul each had served God in great ways, but their focus was not on what they had done; it was on their God. Take a few moments to examine your life and determine what your main focus is. Record your thoughts.

⚘ BEING A BRANCH

5. In order to know God you must spend undistracted time with Him listening to His Word. This is what Mary did. We have addressed the necessity of abiding in each chapter, but now it is time to study it. From your careful reading of John 15:1-17, fill in these columns.

The Conditions for Abiding	The Blessings of Abiding

Jesus spoke clearly and passionately about abiding. As you review this passage, write your definition of abiding.

The Father, the Husbandman, watches over your union with and growth in the Vine. You need be nothing more than a branch. Only a branch! Let that be your watchword; it will lead in the path of continual surrender to Christ's working, of true obedience to His every command, of joyful expectancy of all His grace.

Is there anyone who now asks: "How can I learn to say this aright, 'Only a branch!' and to live it out?" Dear soul, the character of a branch, its strength and the fruit it bears, depend entirely upon the Vine. . . . Therefore worship and trust Him; let Him be your one desire and the one occupation of your heart.[8]

ANDREW MURRAY

6. Synonyms for *abide* are remain, continue, stay, rest, sit, dwell, and reside. With that in mind, what can you learn about abiding from the following verses?

PSALM 61:1-4 ....

PSALM 91:1-2 ....

JOHN 8:31 ....

1 JOHN 2:28 ....

Focusing on knowing Christ was all important to Paul. Take a few moments and write down your thoughts on why abiding should be the one thing that Christians pursue.

The word rendered dwelleth *here is a participle from the verb* to sit, *and here means* sitting; *literally,* "sitting *in the secret place" etc. The idea is that of calm repose; of resting; of sitting down—as one does in his dwelling. . . . Abiding where God abides. The idea is that of having one's home or residence in the most holy place in the tabernacle or the temple, and of sitting with him* in *that sacred place.*[9]

ALBERT BARNES

7. In Paul's pursuit of one thing, he did not allow any past
    accomplishments, failures, or injuries to impede his desire to
    finish well—to reach the finish line Paul effectively used the
    imagery of a race to illustrate how we should live. What do
    these verses teach about running the race?

    1 CORINTHIANS 9:24-27 ....

    PHILIPPIANS 3:12-14 ....

    HEBREWS 12:1-3 ....

---

*Let us then look onward. Let us not spend our time either
in pondering the gloomy past, and our own unfaithfulness,
or in thinking of what we have done, and thus becoming
puffed up with self-complacency; but let us keep the eye
steadily on the prize, and run the race as though we had just
commenced it.*[10]   ALBERT BARNES

THOUGHTS AND REFLECTIONS
FROM AN OLDER WOMAN

Wanting to become more deeply intimate with the Lord is my one thing. Ever since the Lord impressed John 15:5 on my heart, I have felt that the most important thing I need to do is to stay connected to Christ. Only one relationship matters and that is my personal relationship to Jesus. C. S. Lewis wrote, "When first things are put first, second things are not suppressed but increased."[11] I've discovered over the years that the best thing I can do for myself, my family, my friends, my church, and my world is to abide in Him. Only as I sit in His presence can I even begin to produce any fruit that reflects His character. This is the only way I can love, be patient, be kind, and exercise self-control as I relate to others. A. W. Tozer wisely observed, "Yet for all God's good will toward us, He is unable to grant us our heart's desires till all our desires have been reduced to one."[12]

My personal picture to illustrate abiding is "keeping my hand in His." Just as the branch must stay attached to the vine, I feel that if I keep my hand in His, then I'm connected to Christ. He is leading, I am following; He talks, I listen; I talk and He listens. When He stops, I stop. When He is silent, I am silent. Whatever path I am on, I know it is His path for me. Abiding is a lifestyle—a continual communion with the Lord as I keep my hand in His.

Jesus taught that His disciples are known by their faithfulness to His teachings. I think that reading the Bible daily is essential to hearing His voice. This is what Mary did: she sat at His feet listening to His words. My time with God is not always extensive, but I make the effort to sit at His feet consistently. I think that consistency and attitude of heart is more important than the length of time we spend. Certainly morning is the best time to spend reading His Word, but it is not the only time. I have made it a habit to take my Bible and any study material with me whenever I leave the house. If I have not had time with the Lord in the morning hours, I look for pockets of time throughout the day to stop and read. You might take time during a coffee break at work, or as you are running errands, you might grab a cup of coffee and stop for a few minutes to read.

When I had young children, I would spend time with God after lunch when my children were in separate rooms, either sleeping or reading. Since my one thing is to know the Lord, I am committed to find the time to make that happen. I take that time to sit at His feet not because I have to, but because I love Jesus Christ.

Abiding in His Word is a safeguard to maintaining purity of doctrine. Paul's concern for the Corinthians was that the enemy could deceive them and lead them astray from the purity of devotion to Christ. It is only as I read and study His Word that I am able to discern what is true. If a teaching contradicts what is found in Scripture, then it should not be embraced.

So I wholeheartedly and expectantly press on for the heavenly prize. I fix my eyes on Jesus. My life is simple because I have one focus: to know my Lord and Savior. Christ is my goal and He is my prize. I run my race with my hand in His, ensuring my simplicity and purity of devotion to Christ.

🌿 PERSONAL THOUGHTS AND REFLECTIONS

Concentrating on only one thing—this focus on knowing Christ—
does greatly simplify life. Take time to be still and ask the Lord
what might be keeping you from your wholehearted pursuit of
knowing Him. Is there some concern from your past, present, or
future that needs to be laid aside? Write down whatever thoughts
or insights you receive and talk to Him about your desire to keep
your hand in His and to keep "pressing on."

———————————— ᘒᘐ ————————————

*And what is the secret? Be wholly occupied with Jesus. Sink
the roots of your being in faith and love and obedience
deep down into Him. Come away out of every other place
to abide here. Give up everything for the inconceivable
privilege of being a branch on earth of the glorified Son of
God in heaven. Let Christ be first. Let Christ be all. Do not
be occupied with the abiding—be occupied with Christ. He
will hold you, He will keep you abiding in Him. He will
abide in you.*[13]   ANDREW MURRAY

🌿 SCRIPTURE MEMORY

PHILIPPIANS 3:13-14—*I do not regard myself as having laid hold
   of it yet; but one thing I do: forgetting what lies behind and
   reaching forward to what lies ahead, I press on toward the goal
   for the prize of the upward call of God in Christ Jesus.* (NASB)

CHAPTER 6

LIVING IN THE BASEMENT

*When I came to you, brethren, I did not come with superiority of speech
or of wisdom, proclaiming to you the testimony of God. For I determined
to know nothing among you except Jesus Christ, and Him crucified.*
I CORINTHIANS 2:1-2, NASB

*The apostle Paul had a strong and steady underlying consistency in his
life. Consequently, he could let his external life change without internal
distress because he was rooted and grounded in God. Most of us are
not consistent spiritually because we are more concerned about being
consistent externally. In the external expression of things, Paul lived in the
basement, while his critics lived on the upper level. And these two levels
do not begin to touch each other. But Paul's consistency was down deep in
the fundamentals. The great basis of his consistency was the agony of God
in the redemption of the world, namely, the Cross of Christ.*
OSWALD CHAMBERS, *My Utmost for His Highest, An Updated Edition
in Today's Language* (emphasis added)

WHEN MY HUSBAND, JACK, AND I were relatively new
Christians, in our eagerness to grow, we attended many Christian
conferences and spent most of our time reading the latest Christian
books. These are good things, helpful and edifying, but a dear
friend encouraged us that in our desire to gain knowledge, we

might be neglecting the one true source of truth: the Word of God. And this was true. One comment he made has stayed with us: "How do you know that God might not reveal the same truth to you as He has to others?"

I share this story because it is so easy to be overwhelmed with the wealth of information available today. There is nothing wrong in attending seminars or reading books (I write books and give seminars), but in order to become women of simplicity we must be grounded in the basic truths of Scripture so that when we encounter various teachings, we can discern error and maintain our purity of devotion to Christ.

Chambers observed that Paul lived in the basement. Since a basement is below ground level, it is defined by Chambers as foundational—"his consistency was down deep in the fundamentals." The death of Christ on the cross for our sins, the Atonement, is what kept Paul centered. In response to the self-serving, boastful, false teachers who came to the Galatian church, Paul wrote,

> As for me, may I never boast about anything except the cross of our Lord Jesus Christ. Because of that cross, my interest in this world has been crucified, and the world's interest in me has also died. It doesn't matter whether we have been circumcised or not. What counts is whether we have been transformed into a new creation. May God's peace and mercy be upon all who live by this principle; they are the new people of God. GALATIANS 6:14-16

We want our devotion to Christ to be pure—unmixed, unadorned, and uncontaminated. The way we preserve this purity is to know, understand, and cling to the foundational principles of Scripture. To stay committed to these truths we must live in the basement with Paul.

🌿 THE CROSS

1. Paul wrote that though Jesus was God, He gave up His divine privileges and was born as a human being (see Philippians 2:6-7). For what purpose did Jesus come to earth?

   ROMANS 3:21-26 ....

   ROMANS 5:8-11 ....

   1 JOHN 4:9-10 ....

--- ❧ ---

Christ is not one of many ways to approach God, nor is He
the best of several ways; He is the only way, "the way, the
truth and the life."[1]   A. W. TOZER

2. A clear understanding of the gospel message is imperative.
   Summarize the good news of salvation through Jesus Christ
   as given in these passages.

   ACTS 10:38-43 ....

   1 CORINTHIANS 15:1-4 ....

   1 JOHN 4:14-16 ....

2. Paul was greatly concerned that the church might be led to believe
   a different gospel. Record his thoughts about the importance of
   being firmly grounded in the pure gospel message.

GALATIANS 1:3-9 .... ᘒ

COLOSSIANS 2:1-10 .... ᘒ

——————————— ᙆ ———————————

*The Lord alone must be exalted in the work of atonement,
and not a single mark of man's chisel or hammer will be
endured. There is an inherent blasphemy in seeking to add
to what Christ Jesus in His dying moments declared to be
finished, or to improve that in which the Lord Jehovah finds
perfect satisfaction.*[2]   CHARLES H. SPURGEON

THE COMMANDMENTS

3. Knowing the gospel and what God desires for us help to
simplify our lives. Read and record what these verses tell you
about what is essential.

MATTHEW 22:37-40 .... ᘒ

ROMANS 13:8-10 ....

1 CORINTHIANS 13:1-3, 13 ....

1 JOHN 4:20-21 ....

4. Paul wrote beautiful and challenging words about love in 1
    Corinthians 13. In light of the above verses, why do you think
    Paul described love as a "more excellent way" (NASB) or "a way
    of life that is best of all" (1 Corinthians 12:31)?

———————— ❦ ————————

*Every age has its own characteristics. Right now we are in
an age of religious complexity. The simplicity which is in
Christ is rarely found among us. In its stead are programs,
methods, organizations and a world of nervous activities*

which occupy time and attention but can never satisfy the longing of the heart. . . . If we would find God amid all the religious externals, we must first determine to find Him, and then proceed in the way simplicity. . . . We must simplify our approach to Him. We must strip down to essentials (and they will be found to be blessedly few).[3]   A . W . T O Z E R

🌿 BASEMENT VERSES

5. We have studied about the gospel and the commands to love. To me these are crucial to understanding and living the Christian life—a "keep it simple but profound" approach to following Christ. Over the years I have collected and memorized what I call "basement" verses. These verses clearly state the truth, are easily understood, and challenge my heart. Read these key Scriptures and comment on the simple truths they impart.

PSALM 73:25 .... ✑

PSALM 119:11 .... ✑

PROVERBS 3:5-6...

ECCLESIASTES 12:13 ....

1 CORINTHIANS 13:4-7 ....

EPHESIANS 4:29...

I have meditated on most of my key verses for at least a year so that they dwell richly in my heart and are readily accessible for the Holy Spirit's use to reprove, correct, teach, and train me. I have asked God to make them an integral and natural part of my life. To complete this section, begin your own list of basement verses—Bible verses that speak to your heart, verses that you love or know that you need in your life, verses that will help you "strip down to the essentials." (You might also want to keep an ongoing list in the back of your Bible.)

MY OWN BASEMENT VERSES..

6. We live in an age of religious complexity, with many crossroads to encounter on our journey. Jeremiah has a good word for us today in Jeremiah 6:16. His concern was for God's people to return to a steadfast devotion to the Lord and to receive rest. After reading this verse, take a quiet moment and look into your heart. Discover what might cause you to "get off track" or refuse to take the ancient path where the good way is. Record your insights.

Ask for the old paths, the paths prescribed by the law of God, the written word, that true standard of antiquity. Ask for the paths that the patriarchs traveled in before you, Abraham, and Isaac, and Jacob; and, as you hope to inherit the promises made to them, tread in their steps. Ask for the old paths,

"Where is the good way?" *We must not be guided merely by antiquity, as if the plea of prescription and long usage were alone sufficient to justify our path.* No, there is an old way which wicked men had trodden. *But when we ask for the old paths, it is only in order to find out the good way, the way that all the saints in all ages have walked in.*[4]

MATTHEW HENRY

THOUGHTS AND REFLECTIONS FROM AN OLDER WOMAN

I have always liked what Mark Twain said about the Bible: "It ain't those parts of the Bible that I can't understand that bother me, it is the parts that I do understand."[5] King David had a similar thought in Psalm 131:1: "I don't concern myself with matters too great or too awesome for me to grasp." For many years I have rested in this thought. There is enough in the Bible that I do understand and it is more than enough to train and correct me. I continue to grow in my knowledge and understanding of God, of course, but I am content to obey what I do know at the present and not worry about what I don't know.

Having a grasp of the true gospel message taught in Scripture is essential to keeping my doctrine pure. This keeps me from being drawn to different versions of the gospel, which usually add something to salvation. The good news is "Jesus plus nothing."

To remind myself of this good news every day is an encouragement. Jerry Bridges writes, "This then is the gospel with which we need to become thoroughly familiar and that we need to preach to ourselves every day."[6] What this means is that each day I thank God for His great love and sacrifice on my behalf. I thank Him that the power of sin has been broken and I now have the choice of living righteously. I thank Him also that His Holy Spirit dwells within me to teach, correct, and guide me in the way I should go. *Thank You, Lord, for this precious good news.*

Just as the gospel is foundational to our lives, so is the command to love. The only commands that the Lord has for us are to love. A few years ago I concluded that love is not optional for Christians. Love should be my basic and motivating factor. Whenever I am doubtful about what I should do in a relationship, my first inclination should be to respond with biblical love. For me, this simplifies my life.

The essential furnishings in my basement are the good news of the gospel and the commands to love. Other accessories complement these pieces, but these two fundamental truths enable me to keep my hand in His so that I'm always led along the old, well-trodden road that provides rest. I like living in the basement because it keeps me rooted and grounded in the precious foundational truths of Scripture. These truths give the necessary underlying consistency to keep me living simply and purely in devotion to Christ.

❧ PERSONAL THOUGHTS AND REFLECTIONS

Throughout our study, we have seen Paul concerned about false teachers leading the church astray from the truth. This is to be our concern also. We are on firm ground when we stand at the foot of the cross. We cannot help but love when we begin to comprehend God's love for us in sending His Son to die for us. Perhaps it is time for you to make a move to the basement. It is a place that brings simplicity and rest to your walk with God. Take some time to be still and ask God to speak to your heart about what key truths are most important to you. Ask Him to reveal to you what might tempt you away from the basement. Write down whatever thoughts you receive from the Lord and ask Him to give you a strong and steady consistency in your life because of the Cross.

If I covet any place on earth but the dust at the foot of the Cross, then I know nothing of Calvary love.[7]

AMY CARMICHAEL

❧ SCRIPTURE MEMORY

1 CORINTHIANS 2:1-2—*When I came to you, brethren, I did not come with superiority of speech or of wisdom, proclaiming to you the testimony of God. For I determined to know nothing among you except Jesus Christ, and Him crucified. (NASB)*

CHAPTER 7

THE FREEDOM OF ABANDONMENT

*My old self has been crucified with Christ. It is no longer I who live, but
Christ lives in me. So I live in this earthly body by trusting in the Son of
God, who loved me and gave himself for me.*
GALATIANS 2:20

*In our abandonment we give ourselves over to God just as God gave
Himself for us, without any calculation.*
OSWALD CHAMBERS, *My Utmost for His Highest*

EARLY IN MY SPEAKING CAREER I met Carol. She was a women's
ministry director, and we have kept in touch over the years. I would
like to share her present journey:

In 1997, I had melanoma of the retina. Just prior to
discovering that I had cancer in my eye, the Lord God clearly
showed me that I had a hard storm coming, but would come
through it successfully. Today, I am facing the return of that
cancer, this time in my lungs and liver . . . a much wilder
storm. In His grace, God has carefully equipped me for this
climb. . . . I am surrounded by many [family and friends]
who will be the physical arms and legs of God caring for me.

However, the greatest equipping comes from God who
has been my strength since my childhood. He designed

my life, knowing this day was coming. He has soaked me in His Word. This summer, I have been on a quest to deepen my faith. Little did I know that God had a purpose in leading me in this direction.

Today Carol is living in her earthly body by trusting in Christ. She has abandoned herself to God. To *abandon* means to yield (oneself) without restraint. It is to relinquish, surrender, and submit.[1] Because of Carol's surrender of her life, she is free to love God and to have the peace that the world cannot give.

The apostle Paul also was abandoned to God. He told the Galatians, "The life you see me living is not 'mine,' but it is lived by faith in the Son of God, who loved me and gave himself for me" (Galatians 2:20, MSG). To the saints in Rome he described himself as a "slave of Christ Jesus" (Romans 1:1). A slave is someone who is under authority and who lives to serve his master. This is an apt description of Paul's life; it is why he pressed on for the upward call of God in Christ Jesus.

Abandonment gives freedom and simplicity. Once we lay aside our old sinful nature, "which is corrupted by lust and deception," then we are free "to be like God—truly righteous and holy" (Ephesians 4:22, 24).

❦ CRUCIFIED WITH CHRIST

1. Because of Christ's sacrifice, Paul was willing to trust his life to the One who loved him and gave Himself for him. How do these verses encourage you to abandon your life to God?

MARK 8:34-37.. ❧

ROMANS 8:1-4 .... ❧

1 CORINTHIANS 6:19-20.. ❧

PHILIPPIANS 2:5-8 .... ❧

--------------------- ❧ ---------------------

There are three marks of one who is crucified. One, he is facing in only one direction. Two, he can never turn back. And three, he no longer has any plans of his own.[2]

A. W. TOZER

2. Christ died so that when we receive Him we become a new creation. What can you learn from these passages about how

your life is changed when your old self is crucified with Christ?

ROMANS 6:1-11 .... ∂⟋

ROMANS 8:9-17.. ∂⟋

Romans 6:11 says that you should consider yourself dead to the power of sin and alive to God through Christ Jesus. Do you consider this verse to be true in your life? Why or why not?

3. Although the *power* of sin has been broken, we still must contend with our flesh. What help and direction have you been given to resist sin?

JOHN 14:15-18.. ∂⟋

GALATIANS 5:16-18..

JAMES 4:7 ....

In our struggle with the flesh, the Holy Spirit is our special Helper. He knows all the subtle wiles of the flesh. . . . The Holy Spirit is on our side. He is our ally against this subtle foe. He dwells within, where the battle is to be fought. We are not left helpless in this battle, nor are we simply the battleground between these two foes. We are to "walk in the Spirit." That calls for a deliberate choice. We yield either to the flesh or to the Spirit. . . . We must deny our natural desires. We are to do the things that the Holy Spirit wants us to do.[3]   JOHN PHILLIPS

FREEDOM TO OBEY

4.   Since we no longer have to be slaves to sin, we can now freely yield ourselves to righteousness. We can choose to obey—to

do what is right. Lawrence O. Richards wrote, "Obedience is the outward expression of a heart that has turned to God."[4] What do these Scriptures teach about obedience?

LUKE 6:46-49 .... ✑

ROMANS 6:15-18 .... ✑

JAMES 1:22-25 .... ✑

5. God does not force us to obey Him. We choose whether to be doers of the Word or hearers only. The key ingredient, though, in obedience is our love for God. As you study the passages for this question, write down why love is such an important part of obedience.

JOHN 14:23-24 .... ✑

JOHN 15:9-10 .... ᴁ

1 JOHN 2:3-6 .... ᴁ

———————————— ᴄᴗᴏ ————————————

So obedience, properly understood, is never a cold or impersonal thing. God's call to obedience is a loving invitation to experience his best.[5]
LAWRENCE O. RICHARDS

❧ DENYING SELF

6. It is easier to read about obedience than it is to put "shoe leather" to that obedience—to walk the walk. Giving up control of my life seems to be an ongoing battle for me. What are the characteristics of one who has abandoned herself to God?

    LUKE 9:23 .... ᴁ

2 CORINTHIANS 5:14-15 ....

GALATIANS 5:22-26 ....

PHILIPPIANS 2:3-4 ....

The word walk *. . . refers to our outward life, which people all around us can see. "Let your conduct be controlled by the Spirit," is one way of rendering the Word here. . . . Inherent in the concept of "walk" is the idea of making progress. We walk one step at a time. Our progress might not be fast, but it should be steady. We might stumble and fall, but we get up, seek cleansing, and keep moving forward.*[6]

JOHN PHILLIPS

7. Because Paul had died to self, he was enabled to walk in the Spirit. Take a few moments to review this chapter, then write a description of your walk in the Spirit.

Christ died to save us, not from suffering, but from ourselves; not from injustice, far less than justice, but from being unjust. He died that we might live—but live as he lives, by dying as he died who died to himself.[7]

GEORGE MACDONALD

THOUGHTS AND REFLECTIONS FROM AN OLDER WOMAN

My favorite woman in the Bible is Mary of Bethany. I love her not only because she sat at the feet of Jesus, but also because she was abandoned to Him. Evidence of her abandonment is her anointing the Lord with oil even though she was rebuked for her extravagance (see John 12:1-8). What people thought or said was not an issue for her. What was important was that the Lord knew of her love. He was blessed by her gracious gift, for He said, "She has just done something wonderfully significant for me. . . . She did what she could when she could—she pre-anointed my body for burial. And you can be sure that wherever in the whole world the Message is preached, what she just did is going to be talked about admiringly" (Mark

14:6-9, MSG). I read the idea somewhere that even as Jesus hung on the cross, the fragrance from Mary's oil was still on His body.

I was twenty-six when I abandoned my life to God. It was a simple prayer of saying, "Lord, I'm tired of living in my own strength. I'm placing my hand in Yours and now You are leading and I am following—Your will be done, not my will." That was the day I gave up control of my life to God, the day I died to myself. Nothing changed in my life outwardly, but everything changed *inwardly*. I began to realize that the power of sin had been broken. I slowly began to walk in the Spirit. It is a process, but I can say that God's Word is true: it works. When I obey and deliberately yield my "members as instruments of righteousness to God," I experience life as God intends.

I like Tozer's thought that you know you have died when you no longer have any plans of your own. It is a God-given relief and simplifier not to have to superintend my life. One of my favorite verses is Psalm 119:73: "You made me; you created me. Now give me the sense to follow your commands." God is my loving Father and His plans are for my good and for His glory. He does know what is best for me; He created me. Are His plans always what I would choose? No, but I dare not think what my life would be like if I chose my own way and lived as a slave to self and sin.

I think one reason Jesus asks us to carry a cross is to remind us to die to self throughout the day, and He asks us to lovingly obey Him because it is the best thing for us. As Phillips pointed out, the Holy Spirit is on our side and God's commands are given because He loves us.

Bottom line from an older woman: God's way is best. Denying myself, choosing to let Jesus Christ live within me, walking in the

Spirit, obeying the God I love—there is no better way. George MacDonald wisely observed, "You will be dead as long as you refuse to die."[8] Only when I die to self can I truly begin to live.

So we are back at the cross, but this time in a very personal way. It is at the cross where we abandon ourselves and are free to live simply and purely in devotion to Jesus Christ.

PERSONAL THOUGHTS AND REFLECTIONS

This is a difficult chapter. It is not easy to give up control of your life, but what we give up cannot compare with what we gain. Let's not leave this chapter until you have taken some concentrated time with the Lord. Ponder these questions: Have you abandoned your life to the One who loves you and gave His life for you? Does your love for God prompt you to obey? Is your life reflecting the fruit of the Holy Spirit? Are you free each day to say no to your old sinful nature? Ask God to speak to your heart concerning these questions and write down what you hear. Ask Him to strengthen your desire to walk in the Spirit.

Have I ever been carried away to do something for God not because it was my duty, nor because it was useful, nor because there was anything in it at all beyond the fact that I love Him? . . . Not Divine, colossal things which could be recorded as marvellous, but ordinary, simple human things which will give evidence to God that I am abandoned to

*Him? Have I ever produced in the heart of the Lord Jesus
what Mary of Bethany produced?*[9]

OSWALD CHAMBERS

SCRIPTURE MEMORY

GALATIANS 2:20—*My old self has been crucified with Christ.
It is no longer I who live, but Christ lives in me. So I live in this
earthly body by trusting in the Son of God, who loved me and
gave himself for me.*

CHAPTER 8

THE SACRED PRESENT

Teach us how short our life is, so that we may become wise.
PSALM 90:12, GNT

Those who sanctify time and who give time away—who treat time as a
gift and not possession—have time in abundance. Contrariwise, those
who guard every minute, resent every interruption, ration every moment,
never have enough. They're always late, always behind, always scrambling,
always driven. There is, of course, a place for wise management of our
days and weeks and years. But management can quickly turn into rigidity.
We hold time so tight we crush it, like a flower closed in the fist. We
thought we were protecting it, but all we did was destroy it.
MARK BUCHANAN, *The Rest of God*

IN THE BOOK DISTRACTED, MAGGIE Jackson makes these
comments:

Yet increasingly, we are shaped by distraction. . . . The
seduction of alternative virtual universes, the addictive
allure of multitasking people and things, our near-
religious allegiance to a constant state of motion: these
are markers of a land of distraction, in which our old
conceptions of space, time, and place have been shattered.

This is why we are less and less able to see, hear, and comprehend what's relevant and permanent. . . . We are on the verge of losing our capacity as a society for deep, sustained focus. . . . We rarely are completely present in the moment or for one another.[1]

Because we are increasingly on call 24/7, it is easy to be distracted and not completely present for one another. One day I happened to see two women having coffee together, but at the moment I saw them, they were not talking to each other; they were each talking on their cell phones. All too often when people meet, someone is interrupted by some form of electronic communication. We are losing our capacity for deep, sustained focus.

The compulsion we have to multitask can have tragic consequences. A distant relative died in a car wreck because the woman who ran into him was texting on her phone while driving. This is a tragic example of the addictive allure of multitasking. Time is a gift; it is not a possession. It is to be used wisely. George MacDonald reminds us that each moment is to be valued as "The Sacred Present."[2]

❧ THE BREVITY OF LIFE

1. Psalm 90, penned by Moses, is a prayer that God will "teach us to number our days" (verse 12, NKJV). What do these verses say to you about the brevity of life?

   PSALM 39:4-5 .... ❧

PSALM 103:13-16.. ❧

PROVERBS 27:1.. ❧

———————————— ✺ ————————————

What becomes important is not that I manage time, but that
I let God manage me.[3] DAVID W. HENDERSON

2. "Seize the Day" is a common expression. How do these verses
   encourage you to take hold of each day and make the most of it?

   PSALM 118:24.. ❧

   PROVERBS 31:27 .... ❧

   EPHESIANS 5:15-16... ❧

*We must convert our spare time into another kind of time:
time when we study the Bible; time when we turn our
thoughts toward the throne of God in prayer; time when
we pick up a good book, go for a walk, do some gardening,
or visit someone in the hospital; time when we do what we
have sinfully neglected because we were "too busy."*[4]

JOHN PHILLIPS

3. Paul exhorted the Ephesians to use their time wisely, to make
the most of every opportunity. What helps you in making the
best use of your time?

SEEKING WISDOM

4. Considering that Moses prayed for wisdom to live this brief
life, what insights does James give about making decisions
concerning your life?

JAMES 4:13-15 ....

When we realize that our lives are like a vapor, we see that we need to be wise. As you read these verses, write down what you learn about becoming wise.

PROVERBS 2:1-6 ....

PROVERBS 13:20 ....

JAMES 1:5 ....

———————— ❧ ————————

We need to make an active and determined effort to become acquainted with wisdom. We need to make an active and determined effort to get to know the Word of God where the highest wisdom is stored. . . . When we hear and receive God's words, hide His commandments in our hearts, apply ourselves to understanding, and ask earnestly for divine wisdom, we will be on our way to understanding the fear of the Lord. . . . It is a reverential awe that inspires all those who find themselves in the presence of an all-powerful, all-wise, all-loving God.[5]   JOHN PHILLIPS

❧ BEING ALERT

5. Living in the present requires our full attention. As you read these verses, write down why you need to be careful about each moment.

    LUKE 12:35-40 .... ‿

    1 THESSALONIANS 5:2-6 .... ‿

    1 PETER 5:8-9 .... ‿

    Setting our hearts on God's best is a continual discipline. What are the major distractions that keep you from living in the present?

It is important to keep our lamps burning and to be vigilant. What can you learn from these passages about being faithful in the moment?

PSALM 31:14-16 ....

COLOSSIANS 3:1-4 ....

———————————— ❧ ————————————

Think of the things that take you out of the position of abiding in Christ. You say, "Yes, Lord, just a minute—I still have this to do. Yes, I will abide as soon as this is finished, or as soon as this week is over. It will be all right, Lord. I will abide then." Get moving—*begin to abide* now. *In the initial stages it will be a continual effort to abide, but as you continue, it will become so much a part of your life that you will abide in Him without any conscious effort. Make the determination to abide in Jesus wherever you are now or wherever you may be placed in the future.*[6]

OSWALD CHAMBERS

THOUGHTS AND REFLECTIONS
FROM AN OLDER WOMAN

Mary Seel, a lifelong missionary, sent me this note: "Life is good. Did not go to Korea as I had diagnosis/prognosis with liver cancer. As I say with sincerity, God is still numbering my few remaining hairs as well as my days and his mercies and pills are fresh every morning along with His abundant, sufficient grace. All that I need, His hand does provide. Great is His faithfulness."

Mary is familiar with Psalm 90. She lives each moment with grace, wisdom, and humor. Knowing that life is unpredictable, she is embracing God's mercy and provision for each day.

I like this thought, "Time is a circus, always packing up and moving away."[7] Life is too short and fleeting to live it unwisely. Jack and I never leave one another without a "good" good-bye—we don't know what a day will bring. I try to live each day conscious of my mortality. This makes every day precious. It encourages me to make the most of my moments so that I do not end the day with regret or frustration for being distracted and neglectful. It does not mean that every minute needs to be filled, but it does mean that I do not "eat the bread of idleness" to the extent that I allow anything to enter my life that would compromise my walk with God. I need to be vigilant to guard my heart each moment and be careful in redeeming my time.

One way to redeem and sanctify time is to be fully engaged when conversing with a friend. Have you ever been sharing with someone and you knew that they were not really listening or interested in what you were saying? Or have you ever been so distracted by your own thoughts that you were not present for someone else? When at all possible, I desire to have "interruption-free" visits. I often leave my cell phone in the car when having lunch with friends. Unless I'm expecting an important call, I will let the answering machine pick up my calls when I entertain at home. I want to honor whomever I am with by showing them that my time with them is a gift I give to them and to myself.

Buchanan makes an important distinction between giving time and guarding time. One who guards time resents interruptions and rations every moment. Having had a busy household, I identify with this observation: "I have always been complaining that my work was constantly interrupted, until I slowly discovered that my interruptions were my work."[8] Often our days do not go as planned, but when we are abandoned to God, we are free to allow the Lord to use our days as He wants. We need to be realistic in realizing that interruptions are part of life and are often God-ordained, but we also need to be discerning in knowing when an interruption needs our full attention and when someone else's perceived need can wait.

Each birthday I'm reminded that God has graciously given me another year. So each day, each moment, should be accepted in the same way. Choosing to be fully present in the moment is a vital part of becoming a woman of simplicity. This simplifies life because our energies and attention are focused in the present. And there is nothing like the present to live simply and purely in devotion to Jesus Christ.

PERSONAL THOUGHTS AND REFLECTIONS

Wisdom is knowing that life is short and time is a gift. Sadly, many people learn to appreciate this gift only when they have been through a distressing experience. You don't have to wait for a wake-up call to begin to live in the present. Start by being quiet before God and thinking about how you use your time and how you can begin to treasure each moment as a gift from God. Write down any thoughts you receive from the Lord. You may want to end with the prayer I prayed after writing this chapter:

> O Lord, impress upon my heart how short life is. Give me wisdom to live as You intend. Let me be a woman who engages people and tasks wholeheartedly for Your glory. Help me to know how to deal with each day's distractions. Give me wisdom in knowing how to respond to interruptions. May I be fully present in Your presence and focused on anyone who crosses my path. May I learn to value each moment, for it is a gift. May I sanctify each day by living in simple and pure devotion to You. In Jesus' name. Amen.

❧ SCRIPTURE MEMORY

PSALM 90:12—*Teach us how short our life is, so that we may become wise. (GNT)*

CHAPTER 9

THE GOOD COMPETES WITH THE BEST

Dear brothers and sisters, I plead with you to give your bodies to God because of all he has done for you. Let them be a living and holy sacrifice—the kind he will find acceptable. This is truly the way to worship him.

ROMANS 12:1

In seeking the Best we soon find that our enemy is our good things, not our bad. The things that keep us back from God's best are not sin and imperfection, but the things that are right and good and noble from the natural standpoint. . . . Very few of us debate with the sordid and evil and wrong, but we do debate with the good.

OSWALD CHAMBERS, *The Quotable Oswald Chambers*

ONE DAY I WAS MEDITATING on Romans 12:1 and I thought, *Wouldn't it have been better to say "present your heart, not your body, a living and holy sacrifice"? Somehow that seems more spiritual.* A few days later I sensed God's thought in my heart: *Cynthia, you cannot separate your heart from your body. If your body is not on the altar neither is your heart.*

It seems that John Phillips was writing just to me when he said, "For me to be *spiritual* the Holy Spirit must have complete control of me, and the key to this lies in the surrender of the body. For it is through the members of the body that all impressions are received and all impulses expressed. If, therefore, the Holy Spirit has control of the body He can control the whole man."[1]

Because of God's great love, Paul pleaded with us to present our bodies as a living and holy sacrifice. We should choose to do so because it is the best we can give to God.

Chambers observed that it is the good things that can keep us from God's best. Anne Morrow Lindbergh wrote about how having too many worthy activities in her life left her little discretionary time. On a daily basis the good things—not the sordid and evil things—challenge my goal of becoming a woman of simplicity.

We've explored what it means to be abandoned to God, and we studied about walking in the Spirit. Now we need to go a step further and examine how to make wise choices in order to live a simple and pure life devoted to Christ. In this chapter we will address how to discern when the good can be the enemy of the best.

❧ SACRIFICES PLEASING TO GOD

1. A sacrifice or offering was essential in Old Testament worship. But even then God was more concerned about the attitude of heart than the ritual itself. As you study these Scriptures, write down the "good" and the "best" mentioned in each verse.

	The Good	The Best
1 Samuel 15:22	burnt offerings & sacrifices	obedience
Psalm 51:16-17		
Proverbs 21:3		
Hosea 6:6		

There are special sacrifices that please God. Read these verses and note these offerings.

PSALM 116:17 .... ♫

EPHESIANS 5:1-2 .... ♫

HEBREWS 13:15-16 .... ♫

A sacrifice involves a cost by the one who brings an offering. As you review the verses you have studied, write a few sentences stating why you think these kinds of sacrifices please God.

The offering of ourselves should be voluntary. No other can be a true offering, and none other can be acceptable. . . . It implies that he who offers it presents it entirely, releases all claim or right to it, and leaves it to be disposed of for the honour of God.[2]
ALBERT BARNES

2. In Romans 12:1 Paul exhorted us to offer our bodies as living sacrifices. Let's study the context of this special verse.

a. What do you learn from reading the verses that precede Romans 12:1 (Romans 11:33-36)?

b. What do you learn from reading the verses that follow 12:1 (Romans 12:2-5)?

c. What connection do you see with 1 Corinthians 6:19-20?

d. Reflecting on the context of Romans 12:1, consider what this verse now means to you. Write down your conclusion.

Judaism sought mercy by sacrifice and service; St. Paul teaches that God seeks man's true sacrifice and service by showing mercy. We are to come to him not that he may love us in the end, but because he loves us from the beginning. Our obedience to God is to be, therefore, no task-work, but love-work; not servitude, but sonship. God's love is the great motive-power of the new life.[3]   T. F. LOCKYER

CHOOSING THE BEST

3. Since the good competes with the best, then we want to be prepared to discern what is best. We need to revisit some key Scriptures and study them for guidance in choosing the best. Record your thoughts on how these verses help you to choose the best.

MATTHEW 6:33 ....

MARK 12:30-31 ....

JOHN 15:5 ....

1 CORINTHIANS 10:31 ....

JAMES 4:13-16 ....

1 PETER 1:14-16 ....

4. Randy Pausch, the forty-five-year-old professor who delivered "The Last Lecture" before his death of pancreatic cancer, said this, "Things we spend time on inherently take time away from other things. So constantly ask, *Is this the best and highest use of my time?*"[4] We do need to ask questions and prayerfully consider how to use our time wisely. Review your answers from the preceding Scriptures and write down questions that will guide you in seeking God's best for any commitments or choices you need to make, now or in the future. A couple of examples follow. You can fill in the rest.

MATTHEW 6:33 ....

If I choose to commit to this activity, how does it fit in with my goal of seeking first the Kingdom of God?

MARK 12:28-33 ....

JOHN 15:5 ....

If I make this commitment, will it in any way hinder my spending time with the Lord?

1 CORINTHIANS 10:31 ....

JAMES 4:13-16 .... ❧

1 PETER 1:14-16 .... ❧

———————— ❧ ————————

Why are you doing what others can do, when you are leaving
undone what only you can do?[5]
BRUCE BUGBEE

🌿 GOD'S GUIDANCE

5. God's Word provides prayers for God's guidance and assurances
   of His guidance. When you look up these verses, you might
   want to highlight them for future reference.

PSALM 23:3 .... ❧

PSALM 25:4-5, 12 .... ❧

PSALM 32:8 ....

ISAIAH 48:17 ....

⸺⸺⸺ ❧ ⸺⸺⸺

*At first, we want the awareness of being guided by God. But
then, as we grow spiritually, we live so fully aware of God
that we do not even need to ask what His will is, because the
thought of choosing another way will never occur to us. If
we are saved and sanctified, God guides us by our everyday
choices. And if we are about to choose what He does not
want, He will give us a sense of doubt or restraint, which we
must heed. Whenever there is doubt, stop at once. Never try
to reason it out, saying, "I wonder why I shouldn't do this?"
God instructs us in what we choose; that is, He actually
guides our common sense.*[6]   OSWALD CHAMBERS

It is comforting to know that God will instruct us in the way
we should choose. As you look back over this chapter, write
down what has been helpful in showing you how to discern
the good from the best.

⸻ ⤳ ⸻

O Lord, may I be directed what to do and what to leave undone.[7]

ELIZABETH FRY

THOUGHTS AND REFLECTIONS FROM AN OLDER WOMAN

Years ago as a young mom I baked clay Christmas tree ornaments, painted them silver, put a ribbon through the top, and took them to be sold at our women's ministry fundraiser. This memory is vivid because throughout the process, I thought, *Why am I doing this? I don't even like crafts. I have three small children and it is hard enough to cook dinner much less Christmas trees.* As I look back on this experience, I realize the best thing I could have done was to contribute food for the day.

What I did was good, but my choice was not the best. I was stressed because I was doing something I was not gifted to do, and I was irritable with my children because I was stressed. At that time, I needed the counsel that Gordon MacDonald's father told him: "Your challenge will not be in separating out the good from the bad, but in grabbing the *best* out of all the possible good."[8]

The turning point for me occurred shortly after that experience. After another particularly stressful day, I was ready to give up living in my own strength and let God "take over." My description for this is that I gave up "the steering wheel" of my life to the Lord and I moved to the passenger seat. I was no longer in the driver's seat; my life was now His. Once I surrendered control of my life, it became easier to discern the good and the best because now I wanted God to choose His best for me.

Prayerfully using the key Scriptures and questions in this chapter is a good beginning to choosing the best. One caution—it may take time for the Lord to answer or confirm your requests for guidance. One discipline I have is that I rarely accept anything over the phone. I always say, "Thank you for asking me. Let me pray about it." It is amazing what a difference prayerful waiting can make when seeking guidance for what is best.

Other guidelines help me in the decision-making process. One is Chambers' principle of "the good is the enemy of the best." Many times I have taken a critical look at a commitment and concluded that although it is good, it is not the best for me at the time. Another principle of Chambers is "when in doubt, don't." This idea has been monumental in my decision-making. If there is any doubt, again, I must conclude that it is probably not God's best for me. Also I have learned that it is wrong to try to make things "work"—to convince myself that it is right because it is something I want to do.

As a young woman I heard an older woman make this suggestion when confronted with choices to serve: choose one job at a time and do it well. This has been a wonderfully freeing concept for me. When asked to help with some activity, I will say, "I'm serving in this other area now, but thank you for thinking of me." With all our responsibilities of family, jobs, and just daily living, it makes sense to commit to doing our best in one area of service at a time. And now you have an older woman giving you permission just to do one job well.

I don't want to spend my life missing out on God's best. So

most mornings before I get out of bed, I pray, "Lord Jesus, I present my body as a living and holy sacrifice to be used as You will. I relinquish all rights to myself and ask for You to guide me and enable me to choose that which is best. May I, this day, continue to live in simple and pure devotion to You."

❦ PERSONAL THOUGHTS AND REFLECTIONS

When you are able to discern and choose God's best, then you automatically choose your best. To present your body as a living and holy sacrifice is to wholeheartedly give God permission to use you as He pleases. His way is often not our way. He may even lead you to withdraw from some or all active service for a period of time. I would like to encourage you to memorize Romans 12:1. (It is definitely a basement verse!) As you seek to be quiet before the Lord, ask for guidance in walking His path and for discernment in choosing the best. Ask that you may be sensitive to the promptings of the Holy Spirit. Pray that your life can truly be a living and holy sacrifice pleasing to Him.

———————— ☙ ————————

Because I'm less concerned with what others think, my schedule is less crowded with things I once imagined would earn me recognition and fill my empty heart. I now enjoy the freedom to say yes to opportunities that produce gladness in my heart and a greater freedom to say no, even if it's a good thing I've been invited to do. This doesn't mean that I'm less busy. It simply means that there's time now for things I was always hoping before to squeeze into my schedule.[9]

FIL ANDERSON

SCRIPTURE MEMORY

ROMANS 12:1—*Dear brothers and sisters, I plead with you to give your bodies to God because of all he has done for you. Let them be a living and holy sacrifice—the kind he will find acceptable. This is truly the way to worship him.*

CHAPTER 10

PERFECT PEACE

*You will keep in perfect peace all who trust in you, all whose thoughts
are fixed on you!*
ISAIAH 26:3

*Drop thy still dews of quietness
'Til all our strivings cease;
Take from our souls the strain and stress,
And let our ordered lives confess
The beauty of Thy peace.*
JOHN GREENLEAF WHITTIER, "Dear Lord and Father of Mankind"

IN THE MIDST OF A raging storm on the Sea of Galilee, Jesus
spoke, "Peace, be still!" (Mark 4:39, NKJV). Immediately the wind
ceased and there was a great calm. One minute the waves were
crashing onto the boat, the next minute the lake was instantly
calm. This is the power of the Lord's peace, and it is perfect. Our
Lord is the Prince of Peace and He bestows an exclusive peace—a
peace that the world cannot give.

It seemed that Jesus spoke, "Peace, be still" to my good friend
Jane when she was suddenly struck helpless by intense pain and
thrust into hours of confusion and uncertainty. Throughout the
blur of the ambulance ride, attending paramedics, and tests at the

hospital, the peace of Christ reigned in her heart. Like the disciples who were amazed at Jesus' ability to calm the storm, Jane could not explain the calm she experienced during her personal whirlwind.

Whether we encounter medical emergencies or the routine responsibilities of our everyday lives, we need a perfect peace that steadies our spirits and prompts our responses. We need the dews of quietness and the beauty of God's peace. A woman of simplicity is at peace because she trusts God who is her Source of peace and she is willing to step out in faith to seek His peace.

❦ PEACE THAT CHRIST GIVES

1. The source of true peace is God. How do these verses confirm this truth?

    PSALM 29:11 ....

    JOHN 14:27 ....

    JOHN 16:33 ....

GALATIANS 5:22-23.. ✑

2. The Lord blesses us with peace, but peace can also be a result of our choices. Write down what you learn from these verses.

PSALM 34:14 .... ✑

PSALM 119:165.. ✑

ROMANS 8:6 .... ✑

PHILIPPIANS 4:6-7 .... ✑

The essence of peace is inner calmness, rest, quiet, and stillness. When others see you, would they describe your life as peaceful? Why or why not?

———————————— ⨍ ————————————

The unfathomable peace of the God who controls the universe and pursues a faultless purpose, is the peace that Paul commended to his Philippian friends. . . . This divine peace kept Paul's mind and heart. The word translated "keep" in Philippians 4:7 is phroureō, *which is translated "kept with a garrison."* . . . *Between Paul and threatening circumstances stood a garrison. God's peace had him in custody. A great river of peace was thrown like a moat around the citadel of his soul.*[1] JOHN PHILLIPS

3. J. N. Figgis said, "If the basis of peace is God, the secret of peace is trust."[2] Isaiah wrote that perfect peace is for those who trust in God. Trust is faith, confidence, security, and dependence. Examine these verses and record what they say about trust.

PSALM 62:8 ....

PSALM 91:1-2 ....

PSALM 125:1 ....

JEREMIAH 17:7-8 ....

4. God is our refuge and source of our peace. Record a time when
   you have experienced God's peace and security.

———————— ⌒ ————————

*This means that we trust all that the love of God does; all
He gives, and all He does not give; all He says, and all
He does not say. To it all we say, by His loving enabling,
I trust. Let us be content with our Lord's will, and tell
Him so, and not disappoint Him by wishing for anything*

He does not give. The more we understand His love, the more we trust.[3]

AMY CARMICHAEL

❧ PRACTICING SOLITUDE

We are kept in perfect peace, not only when we trust, but also when our thoughts are fixed on God. One way to keep our minds fixed on the Lord is to separate ourselves from the world for the sole purpose of sitting silently in His presence. These moments of solitude can be added to your Bible reading and prayer time or they can be a separate time set aside in order to listen to the Lord. All that is necessary is to be still and pray, "Speak, Lord." Taking time for solitude is a way of preserving and securing peace for the soul.

5. What can you learn about silence from these verses?

PSALM 37:7 ....

PSALM 62:1-2, 5 ....

PSALM 139:23-24 ....

MATTHEW 6:6 ....

---

*We enter into solitude first of all to meet our Lord and to
be with him and him alone. Our primary task in solitude,
therefore, is not to pay undue attention to the many faces
which assail us, but to keep the eyes of our mind and heart
on him who is our divine savior. Only in the context of grace
can we face our sin; only in the place of healing do we dare
to show our wounds; only with single-minded attention
to Christ can we give up our clinging fears and face our
own true nature. . . . Solitude shows us the way to let our
behavior be shaped not by the compulsions of the world but
by our new mind, the mind of Christ. Silence prevents us
from being suffocated by our wordy world and teaches us to
speak the Word of God.*[4]   HENRI NOUWEN

6. Finding solitude in a noisy, busy world is a challenge. As you consider your schedule, what time and place would be best for you to be silent before God?

PEACE WITH OTHERS

7. G. Weatherley made this statement, "Forgiving those who hurt us is the key to personal peace."[5] When there is discord and unresolved conflict with others, hurt and anguish replace peace. As you study these Scriptures, write down what they say about having a forgiving spirit.

MATTHEW 5:9..

MATTHEW 6:14-15...

ROMANS 12:17-21..

COLOSSIANS 3:12-15 ....

Scripture is clear about forgiving others. We must understand that forgiveness is for our benefit; it brings us peace. Forgiveness has everything to do with our relationship with God and our willingness to live His way. God asks us to forgive because He loves us and wants us to be free and at peace. Perhaps you might need to enter into a time of silence before the Lord and ask Him to search your heart. Is there someone you need to forgive, to release? Let the Lord comfort and direct you as you let go of the bitterness and pain that has robbed you of His peace. At the right time, God may lead you to go and seek reconciliation, but first you must forgive and this is between you and God.

Listen to one who learned to forgive:

I do not believe that my family deserves forgiveness, but that is not the point. I longed to be free from the bitterness and rage that were destroying me. Slowly, I began to open myself up to the possibility of forgiveness, and my life began to change. God softened my heart and filled me with love. It was like opening the windows on a beautiful spring day. I believe that forgiveness is part of the healing process and is itself a process. Forgiveness has little to do with your abuser. Forgiveness is about freedom from destructive thoughts and emotions. Forgiveness is about fellowship with God.[6]

AN ANONYMOUS SURVIVOR OF SEXUAL ABUSE

✴ THOUGHTS AND REFLECTIONS
✴ FROM AN OLDER WOMAN

In this unsettled world many people seek an elusive peace, but the only peace that ensures serenity in the midst of turmoil is from the Lord. It is a priceless gift given to God's children who love Him, His Word, and His way. God alone is trustworthy, a strong refuge and a place of safety. It is the security that He offers that gives us peace.

God invites us through His love to come to Him to receive His peace and rest. God really does want us to be alone with Him. He asks us to go away by ourselves, shut the door, and pray in private. Mark Buchanan makes this observation about prayer, "Prayer, before it's talking, ought to be listening. Before it's petition, it should be audition. Before it calls for eloquence, it requires attention. God speaks. We listen. Prayer's best posture is ear cupped, head tilted toward that Voice."[7] This is a perfect description of being silent in God's presence.

Essentially, time taken to be still is a gift we give ourselves, a needed "time out." Basketball teams take frequent time outs to rest, refocus, and receive instruction. And so must we, for we need to stop and catch our breath and be sent off in the right direction (see Psalm 23:3, MSG).

I know that solitude poses challenges: one is to *find the time and a place to be silent*. A time of silence does not have to be long, but does need to have your undivided attention and a heart to listen. We must be creative in finding ways to "shut the door." People constantly surrounded Jesus, but in his Gospel Luke wrote that Jesus often went away into the wilderness (see Luke 5:16). We need to find our own "wilderness"—perhaps taking a walk or going to a library, a bedroom, or a church. One Oswald Chambers saying has guided my life, "My worth to God in public is what I am in private."[8] The other challenge to being still before God is *allowing Him to search your heart*—this can be somewhat disconcerting. Without our realizing it, this can be the reason that busyness takes over our lives, leaving us no time for solitude or time in God's Word. We would rather not have our sin, pain, unforgiveness, or disobedience brought to our attention. But if we truly desire to become women of simplicity, we will abandon ourselves to God and let His Spirit free us and keep us on the right path.

Each of us needs to pray this prayer often: "Investigate my life, O God, find out everything about me; cross-examine and test me, get a clear picture of what I'm about; see for yourself whether I've done anything wrong—then guide me on the road to eternal life" (Psalm 139:23-24, MSG).

It is in steadfastly fixing your thoughts on God and trusting and abandoning yourself to the Lord that you will be kept in perfect peace. How incredibly gracious of God to bless you with His deep, abiding peace. This great river of peace garrisons your soul so that you cannot help but live in simple and pure devotion to Christ.

PERSONAL THOUGHTS AND REFLECTIONS

John Greenleaf Whittier wrote so eloquently, "Take from our souls the strain and stress, / And let our ordered lives confess / The beauty of thy peace."[9] The peace imparted by the Lord is peace that takes away the strain and stress. Jesus has overcome the world and He calms the storms. All He asks is our trust and our time to hear His voice. As you go before Him in silence, ask Him to search your heart and wait for Him to respond—"tilt your head toward that Voice." Write down what you hear and pray for His perfect peace to be evident in your life.

Meditation
    is listening to God.
    is thinking his thoughts with him.
    is the finding of his will and viewpoint.
    is the discovering of truth.
    is giving God a chance to speak.[10]

PETER LORD

SCRIPTURE MEMORY

ISAIAH 26:3—*You will keep in perfect peace all who trust in you, all whose thoughts are fixed on you!*

CHAPTER 11

THE BEAUTY OF SIMPLICITY

Don't be concerned about the outward beauty of fancy hairstyles, expensive jewelry, or beautiful clothes. You should clothe yourselves instead with the beauty that comes from within, the unfading beauty of a gentle and quiet spirit, which is so precious to God.

I PETER 3:3-4

When I purchased the home from Mrs. Crighton, my childhood teacher, she said, "I will sell you my house if you promise to do one thing every morning."

"What's that?" I asked.

"Stop whatever you're doing at ten o'clock," she told me. "Go sit on the front porch or backyard swing and just listen to the birds."

INGRID TROBISCH, *Keeper of the Springs*

WHAT A DELIGHTFUL CONDITION FOR buying a home named in the opening quote by Ingrid Trobisch. It is one that a woman of simplicity would agree to! Although it is not my morning ritual to sit and listen to birds, I look forward to stopping every afternoon to have a cup of tea. It is a time for quiet and refreshment. I heartily agree with Sydney Smith: "Thank God for tea! What would the world do without tea? How did it exist? I am glad that I was not born before tea."[1] This is a special facet of simplicity—having time to enjoy small pleasures: birds, tea, coffee, chocolate.

Mark Buchanan, a Canadian pastor, apparently did not take

much time for tea or birds. When asked, "What is your biggest regret in life?" he thought about his numerous blunders and losses, but honestly answered, "Being in a hurry. Getting to the next thing without fully entering the thing in front of me. I cannot think of a single advantage I've ever gained from being in a hurry. But a thousand broken and missed things, tens of thousands, lie in the wake of all that rushing."[2] Certainly being in a hurry is almost universal. Long ago I vividly remember being convicted about always being in a rush. I was herding our four children into the car when our four-year-old son looked up at me and asked, "Are we in a hurry again?"

But hurry, rush, and overwhelming busyness should no longer be controlling factors in the life of a woman of simplicity. Simplicity, as we have studied, is about living as God intends. It is focusing on living simply and purely in devotion to Christ. When this is our goal, we begin slowly to cultivate an inner beauty—a beauty of spirit that is *gentle*: kind, gracious, and thoughtful, and *quiet*: calm, peaceful, and composed. This is the beauty that adorns a woman of simplicity.

❦ GENTLENESS

1. The fruit of the Spirit is produced in us by abiding. Through abiding we learn to discern the Lord's voice and through abiding gentleness, patience, and kindness begin to blossom. What explanation does 2 Corinthians 3:16-18 give for our growing transformation?

I had a close connecting flight while flying to a conference. I was anxious to deplane and get to my next flight, but I was behind an elderly lady who had a cane and was pulling a small carry-on. She was *slooow*. I wanted to get around her on the jetway, but it was impossible. I hurried to my plane and found my seat. As I sat there taking a deep breath, the Holy Spirit impressed upon my heart that I had just been unnecessarily impatient and unkind. A woman with a gentle, kind spirit, no matter what her circumstances, would have offered to help that dear lady up the jetway by taking her arm and pulling her suitcase for her. "Yes, Lord, a woman of simplicity would trust You for her time and take time to help." How thankful I am that the title of this study begins with the word *becoming*!

2. We become thoughtful and loving because we have abandoned ourselves to Christ and have presented our bodies as living sacrifices. What does 1 Corinthians 13:4-5 say about that kind of selfless love?

The other morning before getting out of bed, I presented my day and my body to the Lord. I dressed in my sweats planning to stay home and write. At the prompting of the Lord, I called my friend Jane, who had recently had a heart attack, to see how she was feeling. As we talked I mentioned that if she needed me for anything, I would be available. She did call a couple of hours later, and after spending the day at the hospital, I took her home and stayed overnight. She kept saying how badly she felt that I was not home writing. I told her that because of my early morning prayer, I knew I was exactly where the Lord wanted me to be.

3. We become gracious because we have accepted the graciousness that comes from God. We are no longer driven by the tyranny of the urgent and are free to serve according to His plan without the irritability that an overly-busy schedule produces. What perspective does Ecclesiastes 3:1 give you in terms of serving?

There have been times in my life when God withdrew me from all or most ministry outside of my home. During one particular season, He made it clear that I needed to focus on deepening my relationship with Him and being available to serve my family. It was the beginning of my "living in the basement" and learning to discern that the good can be the enemy of the best. In this special time of pruning, I learned that patience and graciousness thrive when I am in the center of God's will. It was a necessary lesson that has been repeated, but crucial in my learning that simplicity, quiet, and rest are truly God's way.

QUIETNESS

4. We can be truly quiet and peaceful only when we trust God with all our hearts. Read Psalm 59:16-17 and write down how you are encouraged to trust the Lord.

A few years ago Jack and I were on a flight from Washington, DC, to Tucson. We left late in the afternoon and had a stopover in Dallas. Our plane out of DC was delayed and it was becoming evident that we would miss the last flight out from Dallas. As I rechecked our itinerary, I realized the plane we were already on was the one scheduled to go to Tucson. I gave a great sigh of relief and was no longer worried. As I sat there thanking the Lord for this blessing I heard His thoughts, *Cynthia, this is what it means to trust Me. Because you are My child, you are always on the right plane. You do not need to worry about making it to your destination. You are not to be anxious for anything because I am your Shepherd who is with you and who guides you along the right path.*

5. We can be calm and peaceful because we take time to be still in the presence of the Lord. David's response to God is a good way for us to enter into His presence. Read Psalm 27:8 and write down David's prayer.

Perhaps it is because I am older that I tend to seek out and appreciate the gift of silence, but then it may not have to do with age. Read what my young friend, Michele, has to say about solitude:

> I was challenged by an article to spend five to ten minutes in silence before God each day. . . . I would sit quietly and try to focus on the Lord. Sometimes I would hear nothing and feel like it was a waste of time, but over the course of a few weeks, I began to have the "need" to spend quiet time alone with Him. . . . It was different from my normal prayer time because the only thing I would say is, at the beginning of my time, "Lord, speak to me, Your servant is listening." And then I would be still and quiet and wait.
>
> I remember one of the first times when I was doing this and all of a sudden I realized I was hearing the ticking of the clock. It was so amazing to me that the clock had been ticking every second of every day I had lived in that house, but I hadn't heard it. I had been too busy, my mind too cluttered, to hear the ticking of the clock. And the Lord spoke to me in my heart that day and made me understand that there were many more things that I had missed because I wasn't spending time in silence with only Him. I don't want to miss out on anything the Lord wants to tell me; I want to be able to hear His still, small voice.[3]

🌿 REST
_____

6. We are able to lead a more peaceful and God-paced life when we recognize that the good can be the enemy of the best. Becoming wise and choosing the best is a great step toward simplicity. Sometimes the best is taking time to rest. What do Exodus 23:12 and 34:21 have to say about rest for you and your household?

Jesus confirmed that the Sabbath, a day of rest instituted by God, was made for us (see Mark 2:27). Christians now set aside the Lord's Day for worship, for our rest is not in a day, but in a Person. While many of us no longer practice Sabbath-keeping, I nevertheless think that as we observe the rhythm of God, we would be wise to rest one day a week.

I do my best to schedule one day where I do not *have* to do anything. It doesn't mean that I sit all day and do nothing, but I avoid pressing appointments or obligations for that particular day. For me, at my season in life, it is a day for quiet, for extended time with God, or for time with a friend. I know what it is like to have children, activities, work, etc., but even with your family, do what you can to keep a day that is commitment free. I think that this is God's way for us to manage stress—to stop and rest from our labor one day a week.

7. It is hard for me to be patient or calm when I am tired. If we are to be women with a gentle and quiet spirit, we need to be good stewards of our bodies by getting enough sleep. What does the psalmist have to say about sleep in Psalm 127:2?

I always marvel at Peter's peaceful sleep when he was in prison awaiting execution. Acts 12:7 tells us, "Suddenly, there was a bright light in the cell, and an angel of the Lord stood before Peter. The angel struck him on the side to awaken him." This is an incredible picture of peace because on the night before he was to die, he was in a deep sleep and was at peace. God's perfect peace in our hearts enables us to rest physically.

🌿 CONTENTMENT

8. Quietness is greatly facilitated by an ordered environment. Since the world is too much with us, we need to keep the world of our home as manageable as possible. "There are two ways to get enough," G. K. Chesterton has pointed out. "One is to continue to accumulate more and more. The other is to desire less."[4] What does Hebrews 13:5 have to say about possessions?

———————— ❧ ————————

Everything we own owns us. It takes time to use it, dust it, paint it, maintain it, build space in the house for it, and work to pay for it. . . . Every thing has the potential to become a hindrance to "fixing our eyes on Jesus."[5]

RICHARD SWENSON

9. From the beginning of our study, abiding in Christ has been emphasized as the lifestyle of a woman of simplicity. Oswald Chambers said, "Every now and again, our Lord lets us see what we would be like if it were not for Himself; it is a justification of what He said—'Without Me ye can do nothing.' That is why the bedrock of Christianity is personal, passionate devotion to the Lord Jesus."[6] How does Isaiah 30:18 encourage you abide in Him?

THOUGHTS AND REFLECTIONS
FROM AN OLDER WOMAN

As a woman living in an "image is everything world," it is freeing to pursue the beauty that simplicity bestows. Only in seeking first the Kingdom of God and abiding in Him can I have the loveliness of a gentle and quiet spirit. My spirit is adorned by studying God's truths, living in the basement, growing in my knowledge of Christ, and resting by peaceful streams. The beauty of peace graces my life because I stop to listen to the Holy Spirit who prompts me to confess sin, to forgive others, and to obey His leading. Living as God intends makes me secure and unshakable because the Lord is my Shepherd who guides me along the right paths and provides for all my needs. My identity is no longer an issue for I am accepted by God and have abandoned my life to Him. My confidence and calmness flow from choosing the best and from taking time to be silent. My joy comes from clothing myself with the unfading beauty of a gentle and quiet spirit. It is a joy because it is so precious to God. Because of God's personal care and provision for me, I cannot help but stand in awe that He wants my very best.

I have a unique picture hanging in my study. There is a brightly colored, Picasso-shaped woman tethered to a balloon that has "STOP" written on it. Beside the balloon, these words are written: "Everything changed the day she figured out there was exactly enough time for the important things in her life."

And so my dear friend, my prayer is that you will become a woman of profound simplicity who lives a God-paced life full of rest, peace, and intimacy with the Lord. May your first thoughts and choices be for the eternal, the best, and the important. May the beauty of simplicity, your gentle and quiet spirit, bring glory to God and bless all you love, know, and meet. Keep your hand in His so that you will always be God's woman who lives simply and purely in personal, passionate devotion to Christ.

PERSONAL THOUGHTS AND REFLECTIONS

The Lord has invited all who are burdened, anxious, and tired to receive His rest and truth. He is gentle and humble and when you accept His call, you enter into a life lived in the unforced rhythms of grace. As you reflect on all you have learned, humbly bow before the Lord, be still, and ask Him to give you His thoughts about any changes you need to make in how you live. If it is your desire, tell Him that you accept the offer of His rest. You willingly take His lighter yoke for the purpose of spending the rest of your life living His way—in simple and pure devotion to Him alone.

We simplify, not just to be less busy, even though we may be right to pursue that. Rather, we simplify to remove distractions from our pursuit of Christ. We prune activities from our lives, not only to get organized, but also that our devotion to Christ and service for His kingdom will be more fruitful. We simplify, not merely to save time, but to eliminate hindrances to the time we devote to knowing Christ. All the reasons we simplify should eventually lead us to Jesus Christ.[7]
DONALD S. WHITNEY

SCRIPTURE MEMORY

1 PETER 3:3-4—*Don't be concerned about the outward beauty of fancy hairstyles, expensive jewelry, or beautiful clothes. You should clothe yourselves instead with the beauty that comes from within, the unfading beauty of a gentle and quiet spirit, which is so precious to God.*

The Father spoke:

How are you, My child?

I am well, Father.

Are you tired?

Occasionally, I am tired physically, but rarely is my spirit tired.

What has made the difference?

Your presence, Your Shepherding, Your yoke.

What have you learned?

I've learned that when I keep company with You, I live in the
unforced rhythms of grace. I've learned to take one day at
a time and to trust You with my life. I've realized that only
as I abide can I experience Your rest and live as You intend.

How has your life changed?

I love You more deeply. I treasure our times together. My
perspective toward the world and my involvement in it has
changed, my priorities have changed; I am less fussy and
more flexible. I sense a new freedom to rest, love, and serve.
I am more joyful. I am still in the process of simplifying
my life, but I am on the right path to become a woman
of simplicity.

And what of your heart?

It is at rest. It is set on living simply and purely in devotion
to Christ.

*Good, My child. Surely My goodness and unfailing love will pursue
you all the days of your life and you will live with Me forever.*

About the Author

CYNTHIA HALL HEALD is a native Texan. She and her husband, Jack, a veterinarian by profession, are on staff with The Navigators in Tucson, Arizona. They have four children—Melinda, Daryl, Shelly, and Michael—as well as twelve grandchildren.

Cynthia graduated from the University of Texas with a BA in English. She frequently speaks at church women's seminars and conferences, both nationally and internationally.

She loves to be with her family, share the Word of God, have tea parties, and eat out.

by Cynthia Heald

BIBLE STUDIES:
Becoming a Woman of Excellence
Becoming a Woman of Faith
Becoming a Woman of Freedom
Becoming a Woman of Grace
Becoming a Woman of Prayer
Becoming a Woman of Purpose
Becoming a Woman of Simplicity
Becoming a Woman of Strength
Becoming a Woman Who Loves
Becoming a Woman Whose God Is Enough
Intimacy with God
Walking Together (adapted from *Loving Your Husband* and *Loving Your Wife* by Jack and Cynthia Heald)

BOOKS AND DEVOTIONALS:
Becoming a Woman Who Walks with God (a gold-medallion-winning devotional)
Drawing Near to the Heart of God
Dwelling in His Presence
I Have Loved You
Maybe God Is Right After All
Promises to God
Uncommon Beauty

VIDEO DOWNLOADS AND DVDs OF THE FOLLOWING STUDIES ARE
AVAILABLE AT CYNTHIAHEALD.COM:
Becoming a Woman of Excellence
Becoming a Woman of Simplicity
Becoming a Woman of Strength
Becoming a Woman Whose God Is Enough

AUDIO DOWNLOADS OF THE FOLLOWING STUDIES ARE AVAILABLE
AT CYNTHIAHEALD.COM:
Becoming a Woman of Simplicity
Becoming a Woman of Strength
Becoming a Woman Whose God Is Enough

Notes

CHAPTER 1—PROFOUND SIMPLICITY

1. Anne Morrow Lindbergh, *Gift from the Sea* (New York: Pantheon Books, 1955), 115.
2. *Hebrew-Greek Key Word Study Bible, Key Insights into God's Word,* Spiros Zodhiates, ed. (Chattanooga, TN: AMG Publishers, 1984), 2 Corinthians 11:3, NT Dictionary, 572.
3. Charles Swindoll, *Intimacy with the Almighty* (Dallas: Word, 1996), 38.
4. John Phillips, *Exploring Psalms* (Grand Rapids, MI: Kregel, 1995), 1:175.
5. Augustine, in *The Westminster Collection of Christian Quotations*, compiled by Martin H. Manser (Louisville: Westminster John Knox Press, 2001), 319.
6. Donald S. Whitney, *Simplify Your Spiritual Life* (Colorado Springs, CO: NavPress, 2003), 30.
7. Meister Eckhart, in *The Westminster Collection of Christian Quotations*, 306.
8. Andrew Murray, *Abide in Christ* (Pittsburgh, PA: Whitaker House, 1979), 18.

CHAPTER 2—GRACIOUS ACCEPTANCE

1. Max Lucado, *In the Grip of Grace* (Dallas: Word, 1996), 148.
2. Thomas à Kempis, in *Quotes for the Journey; Wisdom for the Way*, compiled by Gordon S. Jackson (Colorado Springs: NavPress, 2000), 73.
3. John Phillips, *Exploring Ephesians and Philippians* (Grand Rapids, MI: Kregel, 2002), 68.
4. Ibid.
5. E. R. Conder and W. Clarkson, in *The Pulpit Commentary, The Psalms,* ed. H. D. M. Spence and Joseph S. Exell (Peabody, MA: Hendrickson, n.d.), 2:254.
6. Oswald Chambers, *My Utmost for His Highest, An Updated Edition in Today's Language* (Grand Rapids, MI: Discovery House, 2012), April 23.
7. Charles E. Hummel, *Tyranny of the Urgent* (Madison, WI: InterVarsity Christian Fellowship, 1967), 11.

8. Oswald Chambers, *My Utmost for His Highest* (Westwood, NJ: Barbour and Co., 1935), October 3.
9. Artur Weiser, *The Psalms: A Commentary* (Philadelphia: The Westminster Press, 1962), 777.

CHAPTER 3—"THE WORLD IS TOO MUCH WITH US"
1. William Wordsworth, in *A Treasury of Great Poems*, compiled by Louis Untermeyer (New York: Galahad Books, 1955), 650.
2. Oswald Chambers, in *The Quotable Oswald Chambers,* compiled and edited by David McCasland (Grand Rapids, MI: Discovery House, 2008), 74.
3. Matthew Henry, *Commentary on the Whole Bible* (Iowa Falls, IA: Riverside, n.d.), 5:82.
4. John Phillips, *Exploring Galatians* (Grand Rapids, MI: Kregel, 2004), 220.
5. Maggie Jackson, *Distracted* (Amherst, NY: Prometheus Books, 2008), 64.
6. William Morris, in *Real Simple Magazine,* January 2008, 81.
7. John Piper, "Marry. Cry. Rejoice. Buy," *World Magazine,* November 15, 2008, 51.

CHAPTER 4—UNSHAKABLE SIMPLICITY
1. Oswald Chambers, *My Utmost for His Highest* (Westwood, NJ: Barbour and Co., 1935), November 16.
2. Oswald Chambers, *My Utmost for His Highest, An Updated Edition in Today's Language*, December 3.
3. Jerry Bridges, *Trusting God* (Colorado Springs: NavPress, 1988), 32.
4. Lewis Smedes, in *Quotes for the Journey; Wisdom for the Way*, compiled by Gordon S. Jackson (Colorado Springs: NavPress, 2000), 76.
5. George MacDonald, in *Quotes for the Journey; Wisdom for the Way*, 21.
6. Personal letter received from Mary Brumm, October 8, 2008.
7. Jerry Bridges, *Trusting God*, 174.

CHAPTER 5—THIS ONE THING I DO
1. Robert P. Lightner, in *The Bible Knowledge Commentary*, John F. Walvoord and Roy B. Zuck, ed. (Wheaton, IL: Victor Books, 1983), 661.
2. John Phillips, *Exploring Ephesians and Philippians* (Grand Rapids, MI: Kregel, 2002), 143.
3. Andrew Murray, *The True Vine* (Chicago: Moody Press, n.d.), 46.
4. C. S. Lewis, *The Problem of Pain* (Nashville: Broadman, Holman, 1996), 47–48.
5. John Phillips, *Exploring Psalms* (Grand Rapids, MI: Kregel, 2002), 1:369.
6. Ken Gire, *Intimate Moments with the Savior* (Grand Rapids, MI: Zondervan, 1989), 67.
7. Warren Wiersbe, *Meet Yourself in the Psalms* (Wheaton, IL: Victor, 1986), 113–14.
8. Andrew Murray, *The True Vine*, 47–48.

9. Albert Barnes, *Notes on the Old Testament, Psalms,* Robert Frew, ed. (Grand Rapids, MI: Baker Books, 1998), 3:11.
10. Albert Barnes, *Notes on the New Testament, Ephesians to Philemon,* 201.
11. C. S. Lewis, *The Quotable Lewis,* Wayne Martindale and Jerry Root, eds. (Wheaton, IL: Tyndale, 1990), 411.
12. A. W. Tozer, *The Best of A. W. Tozer,* compiled by Warren W. Wiersbe (Camp Hill, PA: Christian Publications, 1978), 39.
13. Andrew Murray, *The True Vine,* 66–67.

CHAPTER 6—LIVING IN THE BASEMENT
1. A. W. Tozer, *Renewed Day by Day, A Daily Devotional,* compiled by G. B. Smith (Harrisburg, PA: Christian Publications, Inc., 1980), January 27.
2. Charles H. Spurgeon, *Worth Repeating,* Bob Kelly, ed. (Grand Rapids, MI: Kregel Publications, 2003), 23.
3. A. W. Tozer, *The Pursuit of God* (Camp Hill, PA: Christian Publications, 1982), 17.
4. Matthew Henry, *Commentary on the Whole Bible* (Iowa Falls, IA: Riverside, n.d.), 4:445.
5. Mark Twain, cited from http://brainyquote.com/quotes/quotes/m/marktwain.
6. Jerry Bridges, *The Discipline of Grace* (Colorado Springs: NavPress, 1994), 58.
7. Amy Carmichael, *If* (Grand Rapids, MI: Zondervan, 1965), n.p.

CHAPTER 7—THE FREEDOM OF ABANDONMENT
1. Britannica World Language edition of Funk & Wagnalls Standard Dictionary, "abandon."
2. A. W. Tozer, in *The Westminster Collection of Christian Quotations,* compiled by Martin H. Manser (Louisville: Westminster John Knox Press, 2001), 60.
3. John Phillips, *Exploring Galatians* (Grand Rapids, MI: Kregel, 2004), 163.
4. Lawrence O. Richards, *Expository Dictionary of Bible Words* (Grand Rapids, MI: Zondervan, 1985), 462.
5. Lawrence O. Richards, *Expository Dictionary of Bible Words,* 464.
6. John Phillips, *Exploring Galatians,* 162.
7. George MacDonald, in *The Westminster Collection of Christian Quotations,* 196.
8. George MacDonald, *George MacDonald 365 Readings,* C. S. Lewis, ed. (New York: Macmillan, 1947), #363.
9. Oswald Chambers, *My Utmost for His Highest,* (Westwood, NJ: Barbour and Co., 1935), February 21.

CHAPTER 8—THE SACRED PRESENT
1. Maggie Jackson, *Distracted* (Amherst, NY: Prometheus Books, 2008), 14, 63.
2. George MacDonald, *George MacDonald 365 Readings,* C. S. Lewis, ed. (New York: Macmillan, 1947), #74.

3. David W. Henderson, "Time to Give Up," *Discipleship Journal,* Jan/Feb 2006, 47.
4. John Phillips, *Exploring Ephesians and Philippians* (Grand Rapids, MI: Kregel, 2002), 151.
5. John Phillips, *Exploring Proverbs* (Grand Rapids, MI: Kregel, 2002), 1:56–57.
6. Oswald Chambers, *My Utmost for His Highest, An Updated Edition in Today's Language,* (Grand Rapids, MI: Discovery House, 2012), June 14.
7. Ben Hecht, in *Worth Repeating,* Bob Kelly, ed. (Grand Rapids, MI: Kregel, 2003), 343.
8. Anonymous professor from Notre Dame, in *Out of Solitude* by Henri J. M. Nouwen (Notre Dame, IN: Ave Maria Press, 1981), 56.

CHAPTER 9—THE GOOD COMPETES WITH THE BEST

1. John Phillips, *Exploring Romans* (Grand Rapids, MI: Kregel, 2002), 183.
2. Albert Barnes, *Notes on the New Testament, Romans,* 263–64.
3. T. F. Lockyer, *The Pulpit Commentary,* xviii:375.
4. Randy Pausch, "Why Bother," *O The Oprah Magazine,* September 2008, 210.
5. Bruce Bugbee, in *Worth Repeating,* Bob Kelly, ed. (Grand Rapids, MI: Kregel, 2003), 283.
6. Oswald Chambers, *My Utmost for His Highest, An Updated Edition in Today's Language* (Grand Rapids, MI: Discovery House, 2012), June 3.
7. Elizabeth Fry, in *The Westminster Collection of Christian Quotations,* compiled by Martin H. Manser (Louisville: Westminster John Knox Press, 2001), 35.
8. Gordon MacDonald, *Ordering Your Private World* (Nashville: Thomas Nelson, 1984), 82.
9. Fil Anderson, "Confessions of a Recovering Strive-Aholic," *Discipleship Journal,* Jan/Feb 2005, 55.

CHAPTER 10—PERFECT PEACE

1. John Phillips, *Exploring Ephesians and Philippians* (Grand Rapids, MI: Kregel, 2002), 164.
2. J. N. Figgis, in *The Westminster Collection of Christian Quotations,* compiled by Martin H. Manser (Louisville: Westminster John Knox Press, 2001), 273.
3. Amy Carmichael, *Edges of His Ways* (Fort Washington, PA: Christian Literature Crusade, 1989), October 9.
4. Henri J. M. Nouwen, *The Way of the Heart* (New York: Ballantine Books, 1981), 17, 75.
5. G. Weatherley, in *The Westminster Collection of Christian Quotations,* 274.
6. A survivor of sexual abuse, quoted in Diane Mandt Langberg, *On the Threshold of Hope* (Wheaton, IL: Tyndale, 1999), 174.
7. Mark Buchanan, *The Rest of God* (Nashville: W Publishing, 2006), 190.
8. Oswald Chambers, *My Utmost for His Highest,* (Westwood, NJ: Barbour and Co., 1935), March 17.

9. John Greenleaf Whittier, "The Brewing of Soma," *The Poetical Works of John Greenleaf Whittier*, Vol. 2 (Boston: James R. Osgood and Company, 1875), 581.

10. Peter Lord, *Hearing God* (Grand Rapids, MI: Baker, 1988), 175.

CHAPTER 11—THE BEAUTY OF SIMPLICITY

1. Sydney Smith, in *A Perfect Cup of Tea*, Pat Ross, ed. (San Francisco: Chronicle Books, 1995), n.p.

2. Mark Buchanan, *The Rest of God* (Nashville: W Publishing, 2006), 45.

3. Michele Husfelt, personal e-mail, September 16, 2008.

4. G. K. Chesterton, "Creating Spaces" in *Discipleship Journal*, Jan/Feb, 2005, 65.

5. Richard Swenson, "I Know I'm Crunched for Time But . . .," *Discipleship Journal*, Jan/Feb 2005, 63.

6. Oswald Chambers, *My Utmost for His Highest* (Westwood, NJ: Barbour and Co., 1935), December 23.

7. Donald S. Whitney, *Simplify Your Spiritual Life* (Colorado Springs: NavPress, 2003), 26.

A Simple,

BUT PROFOUND, THANKS TO—

The wonderful team at NavPress for their excitement and commitment to the Word.

Debby Weaver for her sweet spirit, patience, and insightful editing.

My dear Elderberries—Barb, Deb, Diane, Jan, Jane, and Thompson—for their prayers, helpful thoughts, and suggestions.

Diane, Lisa, Laura, and Zeb, for their willingness to let this study be the "one thing" in their lives for a few weeks. Your diligence and thoroughness simplified the study and certainly made it more profound—you all are a major blessing in my life.

My dear friends, especially Barb, Jan, Marcia, and Trish, who loaned me books, and for Pat and Val, who took time to read through some of the chapters.

My dear husband, Jack, who prayed and lovingly prepared countless pots of tea.

My Shepherd who guides me along the path of simple and pure devotion to Him—how I pray that this study brings honor to His name.

Become the Woman
God Created You to Be

978-1-60006-663-4
DVD 978-1-61521-821-9   978-1-57683-831-0

978-1-63146-564-2

978-1-61521-023-7

978-1-61521-021-3

A goal worth pursuing. Society beckons us to succeed—to achieve excellence in our appearance, our earning power, our family life. God Himself also beckons us to be women of excellence. But what exactly is He asking? If you're hungry for God's perspective on success, dig into God's Word with bestselling Bible teacher Cynthia Heald and experience the joy of becoming a woman of excellence.

Becoming a Woman of Grace
978-1-61521-022-0

Becoming a Woman of Strength
978-1-61521-620-8 | DVD 978-1-61747-902-1

Becoming a Woman of Freedom
978-1-57683-829-7

Becoming a Woman of Prayer
978-1-57683-830-3

**Becoming a Woman Whose
God Is Enough**
978-1-61291-634-7